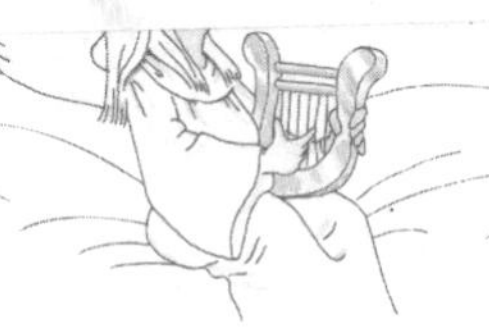

ANGELS MINI BOOK

Discover the heavenly companions in your life

M.J. Abadie

Adams Media Corporation
Holbrook, Massachusetts

An Everything Series Book.
"Everything" is a trademark of Adams Media Corporation.

Published by Adams Media Corporation
260 Center Street, Holbrook, MA 02343
www.adamsmedia.com

ISBN: 1-58062-387-5

Printed in Canada.

J I H G F E D C B A

Library of Congress Cataloging-in-Publication Data
available from the publisher.

Illustrations by Barry Littmann and Kathie Kelleher

Contents

Angels in the Early Morning

Angels, in the early morning
May be seen the Dews among,
Stooping—plucking—smiling—flying—
Do the Buds to them belong?

Angels, when the sun is hottest
May be seen the sands among,
Stooping—plucking—sighing—flying—
Parched the flowers they bear along.

—Emily Dickinson

CHAPTER 1
Angels

What Is an Angel?

There are many interpretations available to answer the question, What is an angel? The narratives in early books of Scripture portray angels as mere extensions of the deity, emotionless and featureless, but later texts indicate they are capable of feelings and have individual personalities.

For example, the angel in Genesis 32:29 who wrestles with Jacob refuses to identify himself by name, perhaps because he didn't have a name? And the angel in Jude 13:18 who foretells of Samson's birth and mission also refuses to name himself. These angels lack personality and warmth; they seem more like robotic minions sent to carry out a job.

However, more personalized images of angels are available. Daniel's interaction with the angels is a good example, as are the fre-

quent statements about Michael and his special duties. Other examples include Luke's narrative about Gabriel and Mary and the journey Tobias took with Raphael.

Looking beyond Christianity, the angel experiences of Mohammed and Black Elk seem much more personal than those of the early descriptions of angelic appearances. And then we have the idea of angels being pure energy or pure spirit. In this context, it is possible to define an angel as a "means through which the Divine is able to give expression; essences of the basal universal force of God [whatever name is used for the Supreme Deity in different cultures]; energies through which God can use as transmissions for whatever purpose He desires."

Originally, angels were not described in any one particular way, neither in form nor appearance, nor in function. Says G. Don

Gilmore in *Angels, Angels, Everywhere*: "An angel is a form through which a specific essence or energy force can be transmitted for a specific purpose."

The more we study angels and how they are, or were, to different cultures, the more infinitely variable they become. For example, the Gnostics, who were influenced by Persian traditions, believed that angels lived in a world of mystical light between the mundane world and the "Transcendent Causeless Cause," in other words, between heaven and earth.

Although, in the Middle Ages, angels, despite the different ideas rife about them, were part of people's everyday life, their influence upon the general populace began to wane after the great 13th century. With the coming of Protestantism, angels took a backseat; Protestants had no need of intermediaries between themselves and God. In fact, that was the whole idea of getting rid of Catholicism, that is, so that the individual worshipper could contact God directly, without having to go through a priest or any other intermediary, including the Virgin Mary and angels.

Although the great Renaissance painters had depicted angels as fluffy friendly winged creatures in the countless paintings of the Annunciation and as adorable little cherub babies with a tendency to float about the heads of beautiful women with cute children at their feet or on their laps, angels lost their previous importance for everyday folk. And by the time of the Enlightenment—with its emphasis on science and rational thought—angels had been relegated to the level of fairies (the stuff of poetry, romantic fancy, and children's stories).

There was, however, one powerful influence that countered the scientific materialism beginning to hold sway with the Enlightenment, and that was of the 18th century Swedish mystic Emanuel Swedenborg, who claimed to commune with angels in his mystical trances. Swedenborg said that all angels once lived as men and women. From his totally unorthodox, but immensely popular, point of view, Swedenborg declared that angels had all once lived as men and women on earth. Now, as angels, they are forms of affection and thought, the recipients of the Lord's love and wisdom.

Following after Swedenborg, Rudolph Steiner (1861–1925), an Austrian social philosopher and founder of the spiritualistic and mystical doctrine known as anthroposophy, developed a complex society of angels and spirits as a result of his own visionary experiences. He was influenced by Annie Besant, who took over as leader of the Theosophy movement after Mme. Blatvatsky's death. Later in life, he repudiated the Theosophist system, but he continued to develop his own.

In 1924, Geoffrey Hodson, a clairvoyant and theosophist, claimed to have been contacted by an angel named Bethelda. This angel gave Hodson information, which he wrote down and later published in five books. Following is an excerpt from *The Greater Gods*:

> *Highest amongst the objective or fully manifested Gods are the seven Solar archangels, the seven Mighty Spirits before the Throne. These are the seven*

Viceroys of the threefold Solar Emperor. A planetary Scheme or Kingdom in the new-born universe is assigned to each of the Seven from the beginning. Each is a splendid figure, effulgent with solar light and power, an emanation of the seven-fold Logos, whose Power, Wisdom and Beauty no single form can manifest. These mighty Seven, standing amidst the first primordial flame, shape the Solar System according to the divine "idea." These are the seven Sephiras concerning whom and their three Superiors, the Supernal Trinity. . . . Collaborating with them, rank upon rank in a vast hierarchy of beings, are the hosts of Archangels and angels who "imbue primordial matter with the evolutionary impulse and guide its formative powers

in the fashioning of its productions"
(inner quotes are from Madame Helena P. Blatavasky, The Secret Doctrine*).*

Hodson further believed that the whole cosmos is guided, controlled, and animated by an almost endless series of "sentient Beings," or angels, each having a mission to perform, and that they are "messengers" only in the sense that they are the agents of cosmic law.

Divisions of Angels

The angelic host, according to Hodson, is arranged into categories, or divisions:

1. *Angels of Power.* These angels teach humankind how to release spiritual energy.
2. *Angels of Healing.* These help humans avoid illness and disease, and they help heal them when they do become ill.

3. *Guardian Angels of the Home.* These protect the home and hearth against danger, disease, and ill fortune.
4. *Building Angels.* These perfect and inspire in the worlds of thought, feeling, and flesh.
5. *Angels of Nature.* These are the elemental spirits that inhabit fire, earth, air, and water.
6. *Angels of Music.* These inspire song and sing praises.
7. *Angels of Beauty and Art.* These give artists inspiration and promote the appreciation of beauty.

The word *angel* is derived from the Greek *angelos*, which comes from the Hebrew *mal'akh*, translated literally as "messenger," and the Latin *angelus*, also translated as "messenger."

Other roots for the word *angel* come from *angiras* (Sanskrit), meaning "a divine spirit,"

and from *angaros*, a Persian word meaning "courier," another term for "messenger."

However, the image of the angel as messenger, which is the most common that we have, and which almost all of the respondents to Don Gilmore's survey thought angels were, limits angels considerably. From earliest times, angels were never seen as single-purpose beings, even though they did carry out messenger duties.

As angelology was originally developed in ancient Persia, from where it was absorbed into Judaism and Christianity, and as the medieval church was extremely disputatious as to what exactly an angel *is*, there is considerable latitude available to the modern person in answering the question, What is an angel?

Whatever ***you*** *think an angel is* might just be the right answer, for people today continue to experience angels through visions, dreams, and meditative states—or altered states of consciousness—just as they have throughout history. Often, the appearance of an angel—usually as a brilliant and loving being of light—is interpreted within the context of the individual's own religious belief system. According to recent research of NDEs (near-death experiences), the common theme is the appearance of an angelic being to guide the dying person through the veil, or threshold, that separates the worlds of the seen and the unseen. Sometimes, communication with angels is done by telepathy, and on rare occasions, an angel may become visible to those nearby the person who is dying. Without a doubt, the angels are there—somewhere, somehow.

Angels in Heaven

"See that you do not look down on one of these little ones. For I tell you that their angels in heaven always see the face of my Father in heaven."

—Matthew 18:10

Israfel

In Heaven a spirit doth dwell
'Whose heart-strings are a lute';
None sing so wildly well
As the angel Israfel,
And the giddy stars (so legends tell),
Ceasing their hymns, attend the spell
Of his voice, all mute.

And they say (the starry choir
And the other listening things)
That Israfeili's fire
Is owing to that lyre
By which he sits and sings–
The trembling living wire
Of those unusual strings.

If I could dwell
Where Israfel
Hath dwelt, and he where I,
He might not sing so wildly well
A mortal melody,
While a bolder note than this might swell
From my lyre within the sky.

–Edgar Allen Poe

CHAPTER 2

Descriptions of Angels

The prophet Ezekiel had an amazing vision of the wheels of God; the vision took place on the fifth day of the fourth month of the 30th year of the captivity of the Jews in Babylon, by the River Che'-bar. In our terms, that was about 560 B.C.E. Medieval scholars derived from Ezekiel's vision the class of angels known as wheels, or thrones, which are the most high. This is one of the most tantalizing descriptions of angels on record.

> *And I looked, and behold, a whirlwind came out of the north, a great cloud, and a fire infolding itself, and a brightness was about it, and out of the midst thereof as the colour of amber, out of the midst of the fire.*

Also out of the midst came the likeness of four living creatures. And this was their appearance; they had the likeness of a man.

And every one had four faces, and every one had four wings.

And their feet were straight feet; and the sole of their feet was like the sole of a calf's foot: and they sparkled like the colour of burnished brass.

And they had the hands of a man under their wings. . . .

Their wings were joined one to another; they turned not when they went; they went every one straight forward.

Angels' Wings

. . . Six wings he wore, to shade
His lineaments Divine; the pair that clad
Each shoulder broad, came mantling
o'er his brest
With regal Ornament; the middle pair
Girt like a Starrie Zone his waste,
and round
Skirted his loines and thighes with
downie Gold
And colors dipt in Hev'n; the third
his feet
Shaddowd from either heele with
featherd maile
Skie-tinctured grain."

—John Milton, *Paradise Lost*

We have seen earlier that the first Old Testament angels appeared as ordinary men.

However, as time progressed, angels took on other appearances, and we have numerous descriptions from various authors about just what the heavenly host looks like.

Ezekiel's extraordinary vision—200 years after Isaiah—tells us that each of the four angels, or wheels of God, he saw had four faces—one of a man, the others of a lion, an ox, and an eagle.

Ezekiel's description of the thrones, with their four faces—one human, three animal—is apparently derivative of the griffins of Assyria from the period 600–1100 B.C.E. These winged beings are also sometimes called genii, (akin to the jinn of Zororasterism). In a cylinder seal at the Pierpont Morgan Library, New York, two genii are seen fertilizing the Tree of Life (700–600 B.C.E.). These figures have bearded human faces, wear helmets, and possess two wings each. However, a later depiction, from 1100–900 B.C.E.

Assyria, shows a bird-headed (possibly eagle-headed) human figure with four wings, doing the same job of watering the Tree of Life. Later, in the 14th century C.E., an illustration for Dante's *Divine Comedy* shows a bird-headed (possibly eagle or hawk) figure with an animal body (possibly lion) at the mystic tree of Paradise.

In an earlier biblical vision, that of the Old Testament prophet Isaiah, Seraphim are described. These angels stand above the throne of God and are awesome indeed. They have lots of wings–six of them in fact. Two they used to cover their faces. Some say against the glory of God, others for shame at human sinfulness. Another two wings were used to cover their feet in a reverential gesture (because they *stand* before the Highest Holy of Holies). The third pair of wings was used for flying, according them swiftness in delivering God's messages.

The biblical story of Adam and Eve describes the cherubims, whom God placed at the east end of the Garden of Eden to keep Adam and Eve from returning to eat the fruit of the second Tree, that of Immortal Life; "Cherubims, and a flaming sword which turned every way, to keep the way of the tree of life."

In later medieval symbolism, seraphim are shown as red, with three pairs of wings, carrying swords of fire, emblematic of their duty to inflame the hearts of humans with love of God. Clearly, the thrones, cherubim, and seraphim aren't what we imagine an angel to look like in these days.

No single description fits all angels. Biblical accounts tell of angels appearing as ordinary men, or as radiant light, or all dressed in shining white garb. Some have wings, some don't. As we have noted earlier, angels with wings only occasionally appear in the Bible. Generally speaking, wings were a later addition, dating from the conversion of Constantine the Great.

Toward the end of the fourth century, angels acquired halos, and it wasn't long before a halo became regulation attire for angelic appearances, especially in paintings and stained glass windows in churches, even though the word *halo* doesn't even appear in the Bible, in which there is nothing at all to suggest that angels possess them. However, since the halo is a great symbol to suggest out of the ordinary beings and holiness (the Virgin Mary usually wears a halo as well), and since biblical angel appearances often involve the effect of radiant light, the halo makes sense.

Wings became standard equipment for angels especially after the Renaissance period, during which the great painter Raphael (among others) displayed angels with enormous feathery wings and benign countenances, marking the beginning of the era of the "nice" angel.

The question arises, If angels have no bodies (as is generally conceded), then are they naturally invisible? In *Angels: God's Secret Agents,* the Reverend Billy Graham speculates that "angels have a beauty and variety that surpass anything known to men."

Is he speaking literally or metaphorically? Perhaps a little of both.

Names of Angels

The names of angels are as numerous as their postulated numberlessness. The least bit of research into this subject reveals not dozens but hundreds of recorded names of angels, and variations of the names of different angels.

For example, the archangel Raziel is also known as Akraziel, Saraqael, Suriel, Galisur,

N'Zuriel, and Uriel. The seraph Semyaza's variations are Samiaza, Shemhazai, Amezyarak, Azael, Azaziel, and Uzza. Metatron had a mystery name—Bizbul—but he had over a hundred other names as well.

The Seven Heavens

In Hebrew terms and lore, there are seven heavens, as well as seven archangels:

1. The first heaven is called Shamayim, and it is ruled over by Gabriel.
2. The second heaven is called Raqia, co-ruled by Zachariel and Raphael. Raphael is considered to be a great healing angel in the Near East.
3. The third heaven is called Shehaqim, whose chief ruler is Anahel. The Garden of Eden with its Tree of Life is found in the third heaven.

4. The fourth heaven is called Machonon, and its ruler is Michael. One of the oldest shrines in Turkey is dedicated to Michael, whom the Turkish people consider to be a great healer.
5. The fifth heaven is called Mathey, ruled by Sandalphon.
6. The sixth heaven is called Zebul, and it has three rulers. The main ruler is Zachiel, who has two subordinates, Zebul, who rules during the day, and Sabath, who rules the night.
7. The seventh heaven is called Araboth, and it is ruled by Cassiel.

The Seven Archangels

The earliest reference to the seven archangels is found in the Ethiopic Enoch; the order varies from what we are accustomed to:

1. Uriel
2. Raphael
3. Raguel (also Ruhiel, Ruagel, Ruahel)
4. Michael
5. Zerachiel (also Araqael)
6. Gabriel
7. Remiel (also Jeremiel, Jerahmeel)

In the Hebrew Enoch, 3, the angels are listed thus:

1. Mikael
2. Gabriel
3. Shatqiel
4. Baradiel
5. Shachaqiel

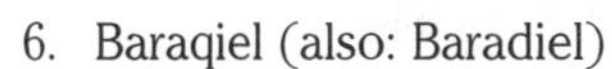

6. Baraqiel (also: Baradiel)
7. Sidriel (or Pazriel)

The Testament of Solomon follows yet another system of names for the seven:

1. Mikael
2. Gabriel
3. Uriel
4. Sabrael
5. Arael
6. Iaoth
7. Adonael

The Christian Gnostics use the familiar order listed above for the first four, only adding Phanuel to Uriel. They then add (5) Barachiel, (6) Sealtiel, and (7) Jehudiel.

The naming system of Gregory the Great also follows the usual order for the first four of the seven: it then adds (5) Simiel, (6) Orifiel, and (7) Zachariel.

The Pseudo-Dionysius order, which was the one adopted officially by the church and which has come down to us through that channel, also duplicates the first four listed above; it adds (5) Chamuel, (6) Jophiel, and (7) Zadkiel. This system categorizes angels into three groupings according to their importance, or closeness, to God.

1. Seraphim, Cherubim, Thrones
2. Dominions, Virgues, Powers
3. Principalities, Archangels, Angels

It is to be noted that in Odeberg's edition of 3 Enoch, the statement is made that each of the seven archangels is accompanied by 496,000 "myriads of ministering angels." That's a lot of angels, and one can only surmise that each had a name.

For our purposes, we will stick with the four archangels that appear at the top of the list that was handed down through the centuries from the final hierarchy of archangels decided upon and approved by the church in the Middle Ages, and the ones who are today the best known to us: Michael, Gabriel, Raphael, and Uriel.

Michael

Michael ("who is as God") ranks as the greatest of all angels, whether in Jewish, Christian, or Islamic lore and writings. His origin is Chaldean. The Chaldeans worshipped Michael as a god-like being, and it is inevitable that the later Jewish concept of Michael was influenced by that of the Chaldeans during the captivity of the Jews there (586–516 B.C.E.).

Michael is chief of the order of virtues, chief of archangels, prince of the presence (of God), angel of repentance, righteousness, mercy, and sanctification. In early times, he was also the guardian of Jacob and the conquerer of Satan, who was still alive and well and causing mischief among humans.

Michael's "mystery name" is *Sabbathiel*, and in Islamic texts, his name is Mika'il. Considered the deliverer of the faithful, he is credited with being the author of the entire Psalm 85. Also, he has been ascribed as the angel who destroyed the armies of Sennacherib (but this feat has also been credited to Gabriel, Uriel, and Ramiel, so take your choice). Michael is supposed to be the angel who stayed Abraham's knife-wielding hand at the throat of his young son Isaac, forbidding the sacrifice of the child. (This deliverance has also been described as the work of other angels, especially Tadhiel and Metatron.) In Jewish lore, Michael is identified as the burning bush that guided Moses in the desert. Talmudic comment Berakot 35, on Genesis 18:1–10, accords Michael as one of the three "men" who visited Sarah to announce she would have a child.

Michael has also been equated with the Holy Ghost and the third part of the Trinity; early Muslim tradition places Michael in the seventh heaven, with brilliant green wings the color of emeralds. To Christians, St. Michael is the benevolent angel of death, delivering the souls of the faithful to the immortal realm and the eternal light.

Gabriel

Gabriel ("God is my strength") is the second highest ranking angel in the literature of all three of the major monotheistic religions–Judaism, Christianity, and Islam. The angel of annunciation, resurrection, mercy, vengeance, death, and revelation, he is an extremely busy angel with status to match.

The name Gabriel is of Chaldean origin and was not known to the Jews prior to the Captivity, but they took him up with enthusiasm. In Midrash *Eleh Ezkerah*, for example, Gabriel is a major figure in the tale of the 10 martyrs (Jewish savants). One of these, Rabbi Ishmael, travels to heaven to inquire of Gabriel why they must die. He is told that they must atone for the sin of the 10 sons of Jacob, who sold Joseph into slavery.

Gabriel is the only other angel, apart from Michael, who is mentioned by name in the Old Testament (except for the Book of Tobit, considered apocryphal). Gabriel, in addition to having been the angel of the annunciation to Mary of her impending pregnancy, presides over Paradise. As the ruling prince of the first heaven in Judaic lore, he is said to sit on the left-hand side of God. (Presumably, Michael, who is a bit higher in importance, sits at the right-hand side of God, although this position is later given to Mary upon her assumption into heaven.)

Mohammed claimed that Gabriel—or Jibril in Islamic—who had "140 pairs of wings," was the angel who dictated the Koran to him, *sura* by *sura*. Mohammedans consider Gabriel to be the spirit of truth.

Jewish legend views Gabriel as an angel of death and destruction—to the sinful cities, naturally, Sodom and Gommorah being especially vivid examples of this angelic fury. Talmudic lore has it that Gabriel was the angel who smote the armies of Sennacherib "with a sharpened scythe which had been ready since Creation" (Sanhedrin 95b).

Elsewhere in the Talmud, Gabriel is said to be he who stopped Queen Vashti from a nude exhibition before King Ahasureus–and his feast guests–on behalf of Esther, who was to have taken her place. No doubt the angel intervened in this scheme because, men being men then as now, it just might have worked, and, of course, that wouldn't have done at all.

Daniel (in Daniel 8) appeals to Gabriel by flinging himself at his feet face down to learn the meaning of the encounter between the ram and the he-goat, which incident is illustrated in a woodcut in the renowned Cologne Bible. Also, in rabbinic texts, Gabriel is the prince of justice.

Mohammed apparently was in a state of some confusion between Gabriel and the Holy

Ghost, but his confusion was understandable considering the conflicting accounts given in Matthew 1:20 and Luke 1:26. Matthew credits the Holy Ghost as the agent that got Mary pregnant, but Luke credits the deed to Gabriel, who "came in unto her," at the same time that he gives her the message that she "had found favor with the Lord" and "would conceive in her womb." Mohammed's interpretation makes one wonder: Could it be that Gabriel was somewhat more than a messenger angel concerning the paternity of the child? We'll never know.

But we do know that Gabriel's was the voice heard by Joan of Arc. According to the court testimony at her trial, Gabriel inspired the Maid of Orleans to raise an army and go to the aid of the dauphin of France, who became Charles VII largely due to Joan's raising the siege of Orleans.

Raphael

Raphael ("God has healed") is also of Chaldean origin and was called Labbiel in that culture. Known as the healer, not only of humans but of earth itself, Raphael is one of the three great angels from postbiblical times. His first appearance is in the Book of Tobit (this text is external to the official Hebrew canon, is cannonical in the Catholic Church, and is considered apocryphal in Protestant Scripture). In Tobit, Raphael guides Tobit's son Tobias on a journey from Nineveh to Media, acting as a companion. At the end of the trek, the angel reveals himself by name as one of the seven holy angels who stand at God's throne in heaven.

The name Raphael means "God Heals," and Raphael is a seraph who is also the head of all the guardian angels.

He is also known as the Angel of Providence, and in that capacity, he watches over all of humanity, which duty is an extension of his supervisory capacity of the guardian angels who each looks after only one human. He is a sort of angelic CEO of the Guardian Angel Division.

As someone who accompanies journeyers on their travels, the trip with Tobias being symbolic of all those who travel, he is related to the Greek god Mercury, who is the patron of travel and all communications. As usual, these attributes are derived from a long line of historical and mythological connotations that have come down through the ages.

As the chief travel angel, he is especially concerned with pilgrims traveling to some holy site or, metaphysically speaking, on the path toward God. Thus, he is seen walking with a staff, wearing sandals (angels often are barefooted), carrying a water gourd, and with a backpack. Raphael is a friend to the traveler as well as others.

According to the Kabbalah, Raphael was one of the three angels that visited Abraham and Sarah. Another Jewish legend credits Raphael with giving Noah a "medical book" after the flood. It is postulated that this pharmaceutical tome may have been the famous Sefer Raziel (The Book of the Angel Raziel), though this book is variously credited in a profusion of concurrences involving a number of angels and at least one demon, Rahab.

Not only is Raphael a seraph, but he also belongs to three more celestial orders, including cherubim and dominions, and powers. As such an important Archangel, Raphael has many high offices, including regent of the sun, chief of the order of virtues, governor of the south and guardian of the west, ruling prince of the second heaven, overseer of the evening winds, and guardian of the Tree of Life in the Garden of Eden, to name some of the more impressive ones. He is also numbered among 10 ten holy sefiroth of the Hebrew kabbalah.

The Archangel Raphael

The Archangel Raphael is known as the Healer of God, and he is the quintessential medical specialist. Raphael's history as a healer shines like a ray of light all the way back to the ancient Near East. As one of the magnificent seven, Raphael is known to have a special healing relationship with human beings, a unique relationship that transcends the ordinarily thought of work of angels as mere messengers.

In Hebrew, the name Raphael (*rapha'* = "heals" + *'el* = God) means "to heal." This word root, however, covers more territory than just physical healing of the sick. It includes all sorts of "fixing" of things as well as people. Other translations of the name Raphael include "to stitch together," "repair," "strengthen," and "pacify." Essentially, Raphael's name implies changing something to better its condition, whether that be a sick human being or a non-functioning vehicle. In a spiritual sense, the idea is to restore to the original (pure and innocent) state of being.

In addition, Raphael is said to be the healer of the planet Earth itself, and today his ministrations are much needed in our environment. We should all be praying to Raphael constantly for help with the enormous task of restoring our environment—our earth—to its original condition!

Uriel

Uriel ("flame of God") is the last of the four top archangels of the holy seven. In Jewish legend, he was the angel of hailstorms (presumably with lightening, since he is called fire), which would relate him to the Greek god Zeus, who had a habit of hurling thunderbolts of lightening when annoyed.

Moses encountered Uriel in the second heaven, and he is said to bring the light of the knowledge of God to humans. His name means "light of God," which presumably equates with fire. Milton named him a regent of the sun (along with Raphael) in *Paradise Lost.*

Uriel manifests as an eagle, and in the Book of Protection, he is described as a "spellbinding power" and is associated with Michael, Shamshiel, Seraphiel, and other powerful angels.

The Zohar I says that Uriel governs the constellation of Virgo. He is said to be 300 parasangs tall and to be accompanied by a retinue of 50 myriads of angels. (A myriad is clearly uncountable. What is the total of one "myriad" times 50?) All of this multitude of attendant angels are made out of water and fire. It's not definite if some are water and some fire, or each a little of both, which seems a contradiction in terms—but, then, much of biblical lore and heavenly constructions is a contradiction in terms. Who, however, are we to question the divine?

Mind you, Uriel isn't the tallest angel in heaven. His height, though quite unimaginable, is exceeded by Metatron, who absolutely is the tallest angel of all the hierarchies. He's a sort of celestial skyscraper.

According to Gnostic lore, which was thrown out by the official church for being

heresy, Uriel is one of seven angels subordinate to Jehuel, known as the Prince of Fire.

Uriel is transformed from Nuriel by a strange process of transformation involving Nuriel as an eagle issuing from the side of Gebura (force) and becoming Uriel. So it is uncertain whether the two are interchangeable. But then, angels have so many different names attributed to a single one that it's nearly impossible to differentiate them clearly, as was shown earlier by the quotation from Gustav Davidson.

Hierarchies of Angels

Why are angels arranged in *hierarchies*, a system of top-down organization, like the flow-chart of corporate management?

There are several reasons why the various religions found this hierarchal arrangement necessary. One was the sheer number of angels. The Jewish patriarchs produced angels swiftly and vigorously. Their method of naming them was simple: Scramble the Hebrew alphabet and add *el* and *iel*. Such angels came to be known as suffix angels, of which there are thousands. The Catholic Church did its best to disband this trafficking in angels, but with little success, as it also named more and more angels. Even the great St. Augustine complained that angels "breed like flies."

Finally, there were so many angels that someone had to get them in some kind of sequential order to manage the total confusion about what kinds of angels did what and which ones were closest to the high throne of God. Since the Bible already had put in place the sense of angels as armies (which is what the word *host* means, as in "a host of angels"), the military scheme was employed, and the angels became arranged in ranks (in the same way that an army has generals, majors, captains, and lieutenants of various grades, and lower ranks from sergeant to buck privates). Mere angels, in this system, are analogous to privates.

Where it all got started was the result of a bit of literary fraud. There had been a famous Athenian named Dionysus, who later became Saint Dionysius the Areopagite after his conversion, by none other than Saint Paul, in the town of Areopagite, Greece, during the first century.

This Dionysius became the first bishop of Athens and a martyr and church hero. Then, in the fifth or sixth century (no one is exactly sure when), along came a Syrian monk from Palestine who produced a series of obtuse mystical books replete with literary allusions and scriptural references. One of these was called *De Hierarchia Celesti.* It discussed in excruciating detail the nature and properties of angels.

However, the Syrian, who wrote in Greek, passed his work off (successfully) as having

been penned by the first-century Dionysius who was famous for having been converted by Saint Paul. He called himself "Dionysius the Areopagite" and duped the church authorities.

Later, around 1450, he was discovered to be a fraud (and came to be known as Pseudo-Dionysius). But by then it was too late, for none other than the great Thomas Aquinas had already put his seal of approval on the hierarchal system that Pseudo-Dionysius had created (as had Pope Gregory the Great, though he made a few minor changes).

Despite his fraudulent identity and the hoax he perpetrated, Pseudo-Dionysius was later sainted! In addition, his angelic hierarchal system endures to this day. (No one has ever suggested that change comes easily to the church; consider that it pardoned Galileo just a few years ago. Galileo, as you probably know, was tried by the Inquisition in 1632

for writing a treatise in which he asserted, correctly, that the sun is the central body around which the planets revolve. The official church position had been that the earth was the center of the universe.)

Saint Paul Ranks the Angels

Saint Paul had begun the process of putting the angels into serried ranks when he was touring the Mediterranean basin during the church's youth, writing letters to the Ephesians, the Romans, and the members of the church at Colossos.

"For by [God] were all things created that are in heaven, and that are in earth, visible and invisible, whether they be thrones or dominions, or principalities, or powers: all things were created by him, and for him." (Colossians 1:16)

And again, to the Ephesians: "Far above all principality, and power, and might, and dominion, and every name that is named, not only in this world, but also in that which is to come . . . " [is God] (Ephesians 1:21).

Though the Syrian monk hadn't been around to hear Paul's actual words, he picked up on them and named the three highest angels, from the Old Testament, as follows:

1. Seraphim
2. Cherubim
3. Thrones

Still using Paul's list, Pseudo-Dionysius further put the angels into three groupings:

1. Seraphim, cherubim, thrones
2. Dominions, virtues, powers
3. Principalities, archangels, angels (the privates)

The ruling Princes of the Nine Celestial Orders as designed by Pseudo-Dionysius are:

Seraphim. Michael, Seraphiel, Jehoel, Uriel, Kemuel (Shemuel), Metatron, Nathanael, and Satan (before his fall)

Cherubim. Gabriel, Cherubiel, Ophaniel, Raphael, Uriel, Zophiel, and Satan (before his fall)

Thrones. Orifiel, Zaphkiel, Zabkiel, Jolhiel (or Zophiel), and Raziel

Dominions (Dominations). Zadkiel, Hashmal, Zacharael (Yahriel), and Muriel

Virtues. Uzziel, Gabriel, Michael, Peliel, Barbiel, Sabriel, Haniel, Hamaliel, and Tarshish

Powers. Camael, Cabriel, Verchiel, and Satan (before his fall)

Principalities. Nisroc, Naniel, Requel, Cerviel, and Amael

Archangels. Metatron, Raphael, Michael, Gabriel, Barbiel, Jehudiel, Barachiel, and Satan (before his fall)

Angels. Phaleg, Adnachiel (Advachiel), Gabriel, Chayyliel

SERAPHIM is the highest order of angels. They surround the throne of God, ceaselessly singing his holy praises. They are the angels of love, light, and fire.

CHERUBIM are the guardians of the fixed stars, keepers of the heavenly records, and bestowers of knowledge. In the Talmud, cherubim are also related to the order of wheels, also called ophanim. Chief rulers are Opaniel, Rikbiel, Zophiel, and Satan (before his fall).

THRONES bring God's justice to earth. They are often called wheels or (in the Jewish Kabbalah) CHARIOTS or the MERRABAH. *Zohar,* the occult book, ranks thrones above seraphim, but other sources place them as cherubim, thus the whole thing becomes confused. The ruling prince is Oriphiel or Zabkiel or Zaphiel.

DOMINIONS OR DOMINATIONS regulate the angels' duties. The majesty of God is manifested through them. Dominations carry an orb or a sceptre as an emblem of authority, and in Jewish lore, the chief of this order is called Hashmal or Zadkiel.

VIRTUES are sent to earth to work miracles. They are bestowers of grace and valor.

POWERS keep demons from overthrowing the world, otherwise they preside over demons or (according to St. Paul) are themselves evil. Ertosi, Sammael, or Camael (depending on the source) is chief of the Powers.

PRINCIPALITIES protect religion. Nisroc, in Milton, is "of principalities the prime," and others include Requel, Anael, and Cerviel.

ARCHANGELS and ANGELS are the guardians and protectors of people and of God's creatures.

A Host of Angels

By the fifth century, there were so many angels' names that a riot of confusion set in, causing the church to declare that only seven angels, the archangels, are known by name. In line with the usual disputation about angels, only four of these—Raphael, Michael, Gabriel, and Uriel—remain constant throughout all the various systems.

Finally, at the Ad Lateran Synod of 745, the active practice of giving names to angels was condemned. The good fathers worried that if angels *all* had names, angel worship would become a problem (it might harken back to the pagan way of naming all sorts of spirits, both celestial and nature), so they decreed "no more naming of angels," in order that only God would be worshipped. Needless to say, the position of the church on this issue has not changed since C.E. 745, nor need one suspect that it ever will. Nevertheless, people are using their imaginations, just as the Hebrew fathers did, and the church's prohibition is becoming about as effective as dipping water out of the sea with a sieve.

As Scripture gives very little support to angels, let alone hierarchical arrangements of them, some modern religionists have taken issue with the very idea of angelic hierarchies. One, philosopher Mortimer Adler, finds such speculation "highly entertaining." And Christian evangelist writer Timothy Jones, in *Celebration of Angels*, states flatly:

> *Dionysius simply had no way to determine if his nine-fold ordering was literally true. Nor do we. Even Paul the apostle, who claimed to have been caught up into the "third heaven" (2 Corinthians 12:2), hinted that such things are not to be told. . . . Indeed, in Scripture, we gain only glimpses and fragments of how the angels might be organized. . . . However tan-*

talizing the recorded glimpses of angels in Scripture are, they are ultimately just that: glimpses. We can take great comfort, however, in knowing that populating the heavenly spheres are creatures so great they boggle and frustrate our every attempt to pin them down.

Angels perform a multiplicity of tasks, some greater and some lesser, depending on the hierarchial rank from which they derive. Their primary duty is to serve God and, by extension, carry out His commands. A main heavenly function is the constant and ceaseless chanting of "glory, glory, glory," as they march in a circle around the throne of God. It is inferred from various sources that the higher orders of angels–seraphim, cherubim, thrones, dominions–are the

ones who constantly praise God and do not leave heaven to perform His chores on earth.

Biblical References to Angels' Duties

The "living creatures" to which Revelation frequently refers were likely cherubim. The Bible's only mention of another form of angel is in Isaiah 6:2: He speaks of the six-winged seraphim as distinct from cherubim. God is said to be seated above the cherubim in I Samuel 4:4, Psalm 80:1, and Psalm 99:1. However, in Isaiah's vision, the seraphim stood above God. Evidently, the duties of these two orders differ: Cherubim are the guardians of the throne of God and act as God's elite corps of ambassadors; seraphim are charged with the ceaseless worship of God, as well as the purification of His other servants.

Other duties fall to the five lesser orders, messenger and guardian angels being the foremost among them, and these duties are manifold.

Angels also serve humans as counselors (or comforters), guides, interpreters, and healing agents, at birth and death, and they give warnings, rescue people, and console those who are suffering loss or bereavement. Angels also function to protect our homes, to interact with the natural environment in which we live, to protect different places (*genuis loci*), and to participate in ceremonial services. They can even act as matchmakers, cooks, judges, and interpreters. The list is long, but these are the major categories in which angels are known to have a hand.

Occult lore holds that angels can be conjured by the adept for various purposes: to strengthen faith, heal afflictions, locate lost articles, increase prosperity, bring fertility, and vanquish enemies. Angels are said to be responsive to invocations when these are performed correctly and properly formulated under auspicious conditions.

Instances of angels performing some of these services can been seen in the story of Hagar, when she was lost in the desert, and in the story of Daniel's rescue from the lion's den, as well as in other biblical tales and legends.

Angels as Messengers

It is a commonplace belief that angels are messengers, that the primary meaning of the word *angelos*, from the Latin, means "messenger." And we have seen earlier in this book references to messengers (of the gods) as angels and angels (of the Lord) as messengers. The two terms would seem to be interchangeable.

Angels as Guardians

That modern Roman Catholic authorities emphasize the role of the guardian angel is powerfully expressed in a poem by John Henry Cardinal Newman, who penned it to express the angel's words of consolation to a soul in purgatory:

Farewell, but not forever, brother dear,
Be brave and patient on thy bed
of sorrow;
Swiftly shall pass thy night of trial here,
And I will come and wake thee on
the morrow.

My Father gave
In charge to me

This child of earth
E'en from his birth.
To serve and save.
Alleluia,
And saved is he.

This child of clay
To me was given
To rear and train
By sorrow and pain
In the narrow way
Alleluia,
From earth to heaven.

—John Henry Cardinal Newman

What Do You Think of Guardian Angels?

1. What is a guardian angel?
2. Does Scripture confirm the existence of guardian angels?
3. Is one guardian angel assigned to each person for life?
4. From what rank of angels do guardian angels come?
5. Do guardian angels rank highest or lowest in hierarchy?
5. When does the guardian angel begin to guard the person?
6. Can a person have more than one guardian angel?
7. What is the most important duty of a guardian angel?
8. Do guardian angels ever take vacations?

Other Work of Angels

For thousands of years, the great religious and philosophic traditions have held that God works through the angels to prosper and protect our planet. The angel makers of early Judaism felt so strongly about this issue that they created literally thousands of angel names to signify the angels that looked after earth. For example, Baradiel is called "the angel of hail," because in Hebrew *barad* means "hail." We have already commented on the making of angels by the "suffix" method.

Because some angelic presences relate to nature, some people believe that the recent increase in angel appearances and interest in angels is an attempt by the angels to raise our level of consciousness regarding the current troubled state of our environment.

Angels, as the landscape architects and gardeners of God, watch out for plant and animal life as well as human life. They also take care of our mountains, oceans, rivers, lakes, rainfall, cloud formations, and the atmosphere in general. And, it is said by some, they cause volcanic activity and earthquakes, which serve as either warnings ("You shouldn't be building houses on this site") or regulators of the planet.

Angels also serve as guides and protectors, as this story told by writer Hope MacDonald demonstrates: A young girl, homeward bound on a bus, found herself being followed by a suspicious-looking man. Terrified, she began to pray. When the bus drew up to her stop, there stood a large white dog, a Great Pyrenees, waiting for her to disembark. As she stepped down, the huge dog put its head under her hand and together they walked the distance to her house. The stalker, apparently wary of the dog's size and presence, took another route. When the girl reached her own door, the dog disappeared. MacDonald has no doubt the dog was a manifestation of an angelic presence, perhaps even the girl's own guardian angel, who transformed itself into a form that would get the job done.

Denise Linn, author of *Sacred Space* and a practitioner of *Feng Shui*, says that there are house angels who serve to protect the home. She says: "I believe that the most powerful guardian for your home is an angel. Calling upon the angels to be your house guardians for protection and spiritual rejuvenation can bring a wonderful feeling of peace, harmony and safety to your home."

Linn, who insists that "angels are real," suggests using an *animal* house guardian, an idea that is related to the MacDonald story of the little girl and the dog. She believes that when we use house guardians, what we actually do is place a protective energy field around our home. I have personally done this many times and find it works well.

This same idea can be applied to *places*, for each particular place has its own angel, and we can call upon these *genius loci*, or "local angels," anywhere we happen to be. This is especially in places we have designed as sacred spaces or in traditional holy spots, such as any of the great henges (e.g., Stonehenge) or sacred burial grounds.

Angels also attend death. The 18th century Swedish scientist-turned-mystic Emanuel Swedenborg, who wrote prolifically about angels, gives an account of how he first encountered "some of the kindest and most profoundly loving of all angels," in what we would today call a near-death experience. He explains that people "wake up" after dying, gradually becoming aware of angels at their heads. These "death angels" are apparently able to communicate with persons who have just died and make them feel peaceful, safe, and happily welcomed to their new state. The transition period, whether it is easy for the dead one or difficult (for some resist believing they are dead), is supervised by these special angels.

As a natural corollary, angels also attend the birth of an infant. Many people believe that the just-born infant is born with an "angel twin," the guardian angel, that accompanies it throughout life. Others believe that there are special "birth angels," who attend the birth to make sure that all is well and then depart for other birthings. A friend of mine who is an experienced midwife has told me that frequently, just when it seems the laboring mother might have to be transferred to a hospital for a Caesarean section, the room fills with a new energy, the woman's contractions become normal, and the child is delivered without difficulty.

After experiencing this phenomenon several times, my friend began to ask other midwives of their encounters with what at first seemed difficult births, and she discovered that many other midwives have had *exactly* the same experience. In a few cases like this, the energy was seen as a suffused light–not bright or glaring, just a comforting glow such as comes from a fireplace or a candle.

The author of *Angels in Action*, Robert H. Kirven, asserts that "spiritual protection of infants is typical of angelic occupations in that it is a kind of service [and that] angels have a special affection for newborn children."

Kirven goes on to say that other angels and spirits replace these earliest guardians when infants grow out of infancy and into childhood; it is a position also held by others, as I have mentioned earlier. The question as to whether the *first* angel assigned to a child is the lifetime guardian angel has never been definitively answered. Kirven bases his opinion on his extensive study of the works of Emanuel Swedenborg.

Angels help with ceremonial occasions, from formal celebrations (such as the Catholic mass) to informal ones (such as weddings and birthdays). Often the receipt of good news, the resolution of a thorny problem, a promotion at work, or confirmation of a much wanted pregnancy is accompanied by the feeling that an angel presence is near and is joyfully celebrating along with the humans involved.

When I am working well, for example, I always get the feeling that "my angel is with me," and when I have a problem to solve, I always ask for help from a specific angel.

Angels All Year Round

January	Gabriel
February	Barchiel
March	Machidiel
April	Asmodel
May	Ambriel
June	Muriel
July	Verchiel
August	Hamaliel
September	Uriel
October	Barbiel
November	Adnachiel
December	Hanael

Angels of the Seven Days

Angels even rule over the seven days of the week! Michael is lord of Sunday; Gabriel, lord of Monday; Samael, lord of Tuesday; Raphael, lord of Wednesday; Sachiel, lord of Thursday; Anael, lord of Friday, and Cassiel, lord of Saturday.

The German lyric poet and writer Rainer Maria Rilke, author of the lyrical prayer book *Stundenbuch* (1905), among his many poetic and prose works, did not neglect the angels. The following is a quotation from *Duino Elegies* (9):

Praise this world to the angel . . .
show him
something simple which, formed over
generations,
lives as our own, near our hand and
within our gaze.
Tell him of Things . . . .

Around our pillows, golden ladders rise,
And up and down the skies,
With winged sandals shod,
The angels come and go, the messen-
gers of God!
—R.H. Stoddard, *Hymn to the Beautiful*

CHAPTER 3

Forms Angels Take

Angels have a long tradition. We don't know if they appeared to prehistoric man, but when history begins to be recorded, we find images of them in many cultures around the world. These suggest that the notion of angels is embedded in our psyches.

Are Angels Real, or Are They a Figment of Our Imaginations?

In *The Reenchantment of Everyday Life*, Thomas Moore describes his little daughter's matter-of-fact question to her parents. "Do you see those angels over there?" the child asks, pointing to the opposite side of the lake. "They're dressed all in white," the girl continues, as if giving a report. Moore goes on to say that he has "no doubt that my daughter saw angels and that angels are as real as anything else."

We know that angels are messengers, and in this respect, they may be like Mercury, who is related to communication of all kinds, or like Hermes, who is a guide for humans as well as a companion.

Recognizing Angels

Angels, then, come in many forms. In *Sacred Space*, Denise Linn says:

> *Right now angels are bridging our physical reality with their pure spiritual energy. Like a leaf falling softly on the still pool of our consciousness, we recognize their presence. As we trust in them, they will pour their blessings on us. . . . And as you become aware of angels they will be more and more drawn into your life.*

What Are Angels?

No one knows for sure, but I believe that they are celestial intelligences–some say beings of pure light–who vibrate at a very high rate, which makes them invisible to us. However, unlike humans, they have the ability to change their vibrations at will and assume material form. When they lower their vibrations to the approximate rate of humans, they become visible to us.

They also can assume other forms and appear as people or even as thoughts and experiences. My own first clear memory of angelic interfacing with my life came at the age of 19.

At the time I was sharing a house with two other girls. The living room was graced by a piano and a Persian rug. On one fall afternoon, I was alone in the house with nothing to occupy me. I lay down on the living room rug in front of the piano for no particular reason, except that I liked the feel of the rug. I wasn't accustomed to lying on the floor, and I wasn't sleepy. What happened was extraordinary, but, perhaps due to earlier experiences with angels, it did not seem so to me.

First, I heard music, as if someone were softly playing the piano, or as if the piano were playing itself, which my logical mind knew to be impossible. Next, I had what today would be described as an out-of-body experience. I had the sensation of being lifted up, up, up, and away; I flew out into the stratosphere, carried by an angel, who held me upside down, by the feet. I knew nothing of symbolism then, but the feet are related to Pisces, which is ruled by Neptune, the planet of higher love and mystical experience.

The angel told me I was about to see my future. We soared on until we reached outer space. The Milky Way was so close that I could have reached out and touched it; it was like a thick carpet of shining stars. From my vantage position, I could see all the stars and planets, and—believe it or not—I saw Earth exactly as it was later photographed by the astronauts. I distinctly remember the shock of recognition when years later I first saw the actual pictures of our beautiful blue-and-white planet photographed from space. *I knew I had already seen it*—just as it appeared in the NASA photographs! This experience would be called déjà vu, or a sense that one has been somewhere one could not logically have been before.

Who Sees Angels?

There are many factors determining who sees angels. The old virtue of "purity of heart" may be the deciding factor, but there are stories of evildoers who, confronted by an angel, gave up their wrongful ways. Certainly children can see angels, and this may be simply because they have not been taught that angels are mere superstition. A child's eyes are open wide to the wonders of life on earth until adult admonitions and restrictive "teachings" cause them to close tight against the miraculous.

What Do Angels Look Like?

They seem to take a form that the person who is receiving their message can relate to. No angel speaks English to someone whose native and only tongue is French or Spanish. Sometimes angels appear without form, as a sense of being given unerring direction. Angels can manifest as a thought in your mind, an urge of your body, or a surge of intuition.

In *Care of the Soul*, Thomas More says:

> *When a summer breeze blows through the open window as we sit reading in a rare half-hour of quiet, we might recall one of the hundreds of annunciations painters have given us, reminding us that it is the habit of angels to visit in moments of silent reading.*

We tend to see our angels as we have had them represented to us through our culture. This variability of angelic presences may account for the ease with which skeptics dismiss angel "sightings" or other evidence of these messengers. But would consistency of form be an appropriate characteristic for a divine messenger?

Angelic presences, or spirits, do not necessarily exist separately from the humans around us. How often do we say to a child, "You little angel!" or to a loved one, "What an angel you are!" How are we to approach angels if they are so variable and mysterious? The answer is *with belief and total trust,* as did the great painters of the past who have left us with so many representations of angels—with wings and without, grand and small, fierce or benign, male and female, adult and child, serene or active, speaking, singing, flying, standing, enfolding, defending, praying, announcing, and playing a variety of musical instruments from harps to trumpets. We must take their reality and their powers seriously and with respect to invoke it in our lives. Thomas Moore says, "Angels . . . are all we have left in our desire to connect with ultimacy and divinity. Without the flutter of their wings in the background of experience, we have only the grinding and purring of machines or the white noise and hum of our own ceaseless thought."

As has been said, angels can appear in many different forms, visible and invisible. Mostly the Christian West associates angels with white-robed, winged, humanlike figures. However, this popular conception of the angel rarely appears to our perception. Often, angels come in human or animal form, or they operate through the agency of a real human.

There is still another way the angelic realm interfaces with us. This is when a celestial energy superimposes itself on someone, who then *acts in the angel's stead*, without knowing the person being helped or why he or she came to be there. When this happens, a person is unwittingly called upon to render assistance and does so as a matter of course, just being "the right person in the right place at the right time."

Angels are less often seen than they are felt—as presences, as thoughts, as ideas, as guidance. Often when I am searching for a reference, a book will catch my eye, and when I pick it up, it will fall open to precisely the information I need. The well-known writer Author Koestler named this phenomenon the Library Angel, and many writers and students experience it frequently.

In *Angels, Angels Everywhere*, G. Don Gilmore says that he believes that "angels are forms, images, and expressions through which the essences and energy forces of God can be transmitted," and that "since there are an infinite number of these forms, the greatest service anyone can pay the angelic host is never consciously to limit the ways angels might appear to us."

Expect a Miracle

"Angels are *there.* You might not see them, but you can always sense them, and when you begin to have contact with your own Higher Self you are likely to have contact with higher beings and infinite energies. The more alert and open you are to these extraordinary experiences, the more likely it is you will find them in your life at some time or other. *Expect a miracle.* And be prepared to recognize one when it occurs. Be on the alert–if you feel the presence of an angel become still and wait for a message. As you become more and more aware of their presence when they visit, you will draw them closer and experience them more often. Many of them are coming closer to the human realm in this period of the ending of an old, outworn, millennium and the birth of a age. They are coming to serve as a bridge between our individual consciousnesses and the ultimate cosmic consciousness which is ready to manifest in all who are ready to receive its energy and message of love and peace to all everywhere. Listen with your ears, eyes, mind, emotions, body, and–above all–with your heart."

–M. J. Abadie, *Awaken to Your Spiritual Self*

Angels, then, come in many forms. How we perceive them will depend on our personal belief systems and what images we have received as children. The classic picture most of us have of an angel is a being with a serene face, wearing flowing white robes, borne on big, beautiful feathered wings, and radiating brilliant light.

This child's version of the ideal was imprinted early on most Christian children, but as we have seen earlier, the Old Testament angels often arrived disguised as ordinary men.

However, in their visions, which seem to have been extraordinary out-of-body experiences or else the product of a vivid and complex ability to receive images or information in a trance state, the prophets and later religious philosophers, such as Swedenborg, "saw" angels as almost unbelievably glorious beings.

When we read the proliferating accounts of people, both in our own time and in past history, we find that there are many descriptions of the form in which an angel can be seen, felt, or in some other manner experienced.

Angel stories in our times are so varied that it is impossible to come to any conclusion. Just as witnesses to an accident will describe different versions of what they saw—or thought they saw—happen (as any law officer can confirm), so recipients of angel experiences will recount surprising, even contradictory, versions of the event.

Our perceptions of angels are ordinarily accompanied by positive feelings. But whether they are perceived as being beneficial or threatening, we tend to accept what we see as being the true reality.

Who Sees Angels the Most Easily?

Clearly the deeply religious or those especially inclined to seeing visions may be the most frequent recipients of angel visitations. However, as stated previously, the angels appear in forms that are familiar to the person who receives the vision. For example, a devout Hindu wouldn't likely see the standard feather-winged white-gowned Christian angelic form; nor would a person who speaks only French receive a message from an angel speaking another tongue. Angels for the most part appear in both the cultural norm and the religious format to which the person is accustomed.

Angels can appear as animals, as they did when Elijah was fed in the wilderness by ravens (those birds flying to him morning and evening with sustenance were angels in disguise). But Elijah, as a desert inhabitant, would not have found ravens unusual.

Birds—quite possibly because they are naturally winged creatures and have the gift of flight that humans yearn for—are often seen by indigenous peoples, such as Native Americans.

A gentleman I once knew fairly closely, who was a blind massage therapist to whom I went for treatments, was at a particularly difficult time in his life. Born sighted, he had lost his vision in his early 20s from an illness, and the adjustment was intense and difficult. One fine spring day, just after he had opened his massage offices in Manhattan, he had all the windows open, and a pair of beautiful birds—brightly colored song birds—flew in the window and around his head in a circle. He, of course, could not see them, but he could sense them. He called to his wife, who was also his receptionist, to come into the room and tell him what was happening. To her utter astonishment, she saw the pair of birds flying in circles above his head. They both interpreted this extremely unusual appearance as angelic, as a message that his new massage business would prosper. And it did. Later, he claimed to be glad of his blindness, as it gave him special feeling senses with which to diagnose and treat his patients.

There are many passages in Scripture that describe angels in one or another bodily form, human or otherwise. However, there are those who believe that angels *never* assume bodies, that all the so-called angelic appearances cited in the Bible were *visions*, divinely inspired perhaps, but taking place in the imagination of the prophet or person who had the vision. Contradicting this are the cases in which the Scriptures speak of angels appearing visibly to several people simultaneously, such as Abraham's servants and the populace of Sodom who saw the angels who visited Lot—and lusted after them as well!

Therefore, it is probably safe to say that angels are incorporeal beings who are capable of assuming bodies in order to present themselves to humans for whatever deed needs doing. Father Walter Farrell, O.P., a 20th century Aquinas scholar, observes that an angel assuming a body is analogous to a man renting a tuxedo to wear to a wedding.

He puts the garb on for the special occasion and then takes it off again and returns to the natural angel state. If this is so–and it seems a likely construct–then the bodies angels assume for their earthly tasks do not operate in the same manner as human bodies–in terms of the usual bodily needs and functions, such as eating, drinking, the digestive and elimination processes, sleep, and so on. The angel Raphael makes this clear in Tobias. Just before rising up and disappearing into thin air, he said, "You thought you saw me eating, but that was merely an appearance and no more."

It seems clear to me that *angels can function in any medium*, be it human or animal forms, intuitions, feelings, apparitions, or–especially–dreams.

What Are Your Thoughts About Angels?

1. How do you picture angels?
2. If you have ever seen an angel, describe it.
3. Was your angel male or female or you couldn't tell?
4. Did your angel appear in human form?
5. If not human form, what form did your angel assume?
6. Have you seen an angel more than once?
7. Under what circumstances did you experience an angel?
8. Did your angel have wings? How was it dressed?
9. Did you see a single angel or a group of angels?

CHAPTER 4

How to Recognize Angelic Presences

What do angels look like? Whatever pleases them or suits their purpose. They seem to take a form that the person who is receiving their message can relate to. No angel speaks English to someone whose native and only tongue is French or Spanish. Angels can manifest as a thought in your mind, an urge of your body, or a surge of intuition.

This variability of angelic presences may account for the ease with which skeptics dismiss angel "sightings" or other evidences of these messengers, as if consistency of form were an appropriate characteristic for a divine messenger! We tend to see our angels as we have had them represented to us through our culture, which is actually as much a form of language as the tongue we speak. And just as languages are modified by dialect, so do angels fit their appearances to the circumstances involved.

The Christian West associates angels with white-robed, winged, humanlike figures. However, this popular conception of the angel is rarely what we actually perceive. Often, angels come in human or animal form, or they operate through the agency of a real human.

Angels are less often seen than they are *felt*—as presences, as thoughts, as ideas, as guidance. Often when I am searching for a reference, a book I wasn't looking for will catch my eye, and when I pick it up, it will fall open to precisely the information I need. Many writers have commented on this phenomenon, which the English writer Aldous Huxley called The Library Angel.

There are many ways you can tell if an angel is around. Sometimes there are sweet smells like flowers, or there can be a slight breeze. I have a hanging Tiffany glass lamp that sometimes sways gently back and forth when all the windows are closed and the air is entirely still. It's a signal that an angel is visiting me. Bodily sensations can also be caused by angels–in the form of heightened senses or in an altered state of consciousness that is conducive to the receiving of messages.

Some people hear sounds–bells, chimes, or trumpets. Some speculate that the sound of trumpets is actually the angels crashing through the sound barrier as they break into our dimension by lowering their vibrations.

Light is another angelic form of announcement. The word *angelos* in the original Greek means "messenger," and in this respect, the work of angels may be related to that of Mercury, or Hermes, one of whose daughters is called angel by Pindar. A daughter of Zeus, Iris—who, as the goddess of the rainbow, represents the magical bow of colored light we see in the sky—is described as an angel by the writer Hesiod. These terms suggest that an angel is a special carrier of messages from the gods, as was the case of the angel Gabriel announcing to the Virgin Mary that she was to become impregnated by the Holy Spirit. In paintings, angels with such messages often ride a beam of light.

The feeling of being suffused with love is another example of how one can feel or sense the presence of an angel. Many others have reported this experience. It can be accompanied by some sort of phenomenon, or it can just well up inside on an ordinary day in your usual routine of life. It's as if ordinary time suddenly stops and we are transported—even if only for a moment or two—into the sense that things are not as they seem, that someone or something is close by, looking after us and *caring what happens to us*. The chances of most of us having a dramatic angelic experience or vivid visionary tour of heaven's realms is relatively slim, but the *sensing* of angelic presence is available to all who are willing to pay attention. The mere fact that angels are all around attests to a myriad of unseen activities beyond our usual conscious awareness.

Ordinarily, we slip accidentally into such experiences, and they are fleeting and

ephemeral. But they can be found regularly if only we become silent and wait for them to appear before our inner eye. These hints of another reality—these momentary liftings of the veil between the worlds—come to us when we are aware and *listening* for their soft tread in our inner landscape.

Silence

Contact with the angels occurs in the quiet stillness, when mind and heart are at rest. This point of silence is comparable to "the still point at the center of the turning wheel." This still center is the gateway between the striving ego and the angelic realm seeking our attention. To find our center, we must become quiet and still. Only then can we thread our way through the usual untidy jumble of our colliding thoughts to that place within where the spirit dwells.

Silence is the road to the center of the self. It is in our silences that we experience unity and recognize ourselves as being part of the All. This is the essence of sensing the nearness of angels. Almost everyone has had the experience at some time, perhaps while sitting by a lake in silence and solitude, gazing at a sleeping child, or caught alone and awestruck by a magnificent sunset on a country road. These are mystical moments that connect us to the larger totality of which we are an integral part. We are transfixed and transformed for the moment. It's difficult to describe the feeling, and we have no adequate words for that sense of having stepped outside our normal boundaries into something grand and inspiring. It always happens in silence.

Often, just slowing down a bit—letting ourselves be a witness to our own multilayered lives—is an illuminating experience. As we progress through our silence to the still point within, we peel away the layers of miscellaneous thought that have impeded our contact with the angelic world that lies beneath our every thought and action. Through the practice of silence we open ourselves to direct experience of the Most High.

Silence is not merely the absence of sound. It is a restful space that we inhabit when we are feeling our most free and uninhibited. Like pointers on a spiritual roadmap, silence leads to the next step we are required to take for our continued growth and development. Silence is a great spiritual master who guides us and illuminates our way when it is dark. In the silence of the inner self, we reach *gnosis*, or truth, and in so doing, we find our angels there, guiding and gracing us, delivering the messages we need to hear.

They Watch Over Us

Now that the earth has gathered
over this generation,
they live upon earth,
and are good; they watch over
mortal men
and defend them from evil;
they keep watch over lawsuits and
hard dealings;
they mantle themselves in dark mist
and wander all over the country;
they bestow wealth; for this right
as of kings was given them.

—*Hesiod,* Works and Days

The angels want to help us, and they want us to be able to recognize their presence in our lives. But often their "still, small voices" cannot be heard through the jumble of sound and miscellaneous thought with which we entertain and occupy ourselves.

Precious Gifts

The teachings of angels are precious gifts to be gleaned from the caves of undisturbed silence deep within ourselves like crystals ever growing because they are alive.

—*Karen Goldman,* Angel Voices

Angels are everywhere around us, but it is our own responsibility to make ourselves open to their presence by eliminating the excess noise we permit and even encourage in our lives.

Demanding silence for one's self in this society requires a major leap of faith. Not only must we overcome obstacles merely to obtain some silence in our busy lives, but we must

also jealously guard that silence against noisy invaders, including the ones inside who may try to sabotage our efforts to be silent. Given silence unexpectedly—whether a few moments or a few hours—most of us apprehensively reach out for the nearest sound with which to distract ourselves. Realize that silence is not the enemy. It is the great mother lode of the angelic realm.

Fortunately, you do not have to retire to a monastery or become a hermit to experience the contemplative silence that is at the heart of experiencing the angelic world. You can achieve your own silence, contact your still center, and recognize the presence of angels by practicing silence on a daily basis.

Focusing Technique

This focusing technique will allow you to make room in your life for the silence you need to detect angelic beings. To do this exercise, you will need pen and paper and at least 20 minutes of quiet, undisturbed time. Ask yourself the questions listed below, sit with them for a few minutes, turning them over and around to get a feeling for how you want to answer. Then, when you are feeling clear and relaxed, make three columns on a page and give each column one of the following questions:

What silence do I want to manifest in
my life?
What noise do I want to get rid of in
my life?
What would be a good balance between
sound and silence in my life?

Now, list everything you can think of for each question, including how you feel about the question itself. Let your imagination roam freely. Don't worry about how you are going to achieve results yet. Staying focused about what you want to achieve is the key to success. Knowing what you don't want allows you to focus more clearly on what you do want. Focusing on what you truly want will activate inner direction.

Solitude

If silence is golden, solitude is a precious jewel. The historian Edward Gibbon called solitude "the school of genius," and Karen Goldman, in *Angel Voices*, echoes the sentiment: "Our angel voices come from a place where we do not think, from a quietness inside us and all around us, from a pristine place . . . perfect within us."

Solitude, that necessary adjunct to recognizing the angelic presences that surround us at all times, is, in our socially driven society, as difficult to attain as is silence. If we fear silence, we see solitude as the ultimate negative state. Instead of being recognized as a treasure-house of sublime gifts, all too often, being alone is viewed as a noxious condition to be remedied at once. And if we cannot fill the empty spaces with living people, the flickering color images on the TV set or the chattering of the endless supply of radio talk shows will do as well.

Yet, like silence, solitude is "the necessary thing." Without it we are consumed in the backwash of others' lives. Lacking solitude, we are lonely despite the presence of others . . . lonely because we are not in touch with our deepest selves. When we fill up our hours, days, years, whole lives with the constant presence of others, we forfeit the opportunity to know ourselves. Neglecting or abandoning this innermost self reaps a bitter harvest. We feel we don't know who we truly are, and indeed we do not, having never bothered to go within where the true self dwells, the self that is open to recognizing the angel within who only awaits awakening to give us a glimpse of our personal paradise. The angels do not conceal themselves from us; we hide from them by refusing the gifts of solitude.

Somehow we feel that the solitary individual is to be pitied as inferior, deficient in some way—unable or unwilling to make "significant" relationships with others. Yet, the world's most creative artists and writers have by and large preferred solitude to company. And the great visionaries whose encounters with angels have come down to us through various sources such as the Bible, the Koran, and other mystical religious writings like those of St. Catherine, have had their experiences of angels alone. The prophets of old retired to mountain caves for days of solitary meditation

before their visions occurred. It would seem that solitude is indeed "the necessary thing" if one wants to experience the presence of angels.

Abraham Maslow, the psychologist who identified *peak experiences*, those moments of feeling total unity—a recognition of the Self in the All—said that the ability to have peak experiences is dependent upon being free of other people, "which in turn means that we become much more . . . our authentic selves, our real identity." Maslow's approach differs considerably from those who propose that the entire meaning of life is derived from interpersonal relationships.

Complete happiness, that oceanic feeling of perfect harmony between the inner and outer worlds is at best an infrequent experience, but the most profound psychological and spiritual experiences invariably take place internally, witnessed only by the "indwelling self." Rarely, and then only distantly, are these experiences related to interaction with other human beings. Human adaptation to the world is largely a product of the imagination and the development of an inner world in which to shield the self from the vagaries of the outer world. Without this inner world, without a strong and well-built structure within, the outer world seems threatening and dangerous. The ability to remove one's self, to be "totally immersed, fascinated, and absorbed in the present, in the here and now, enables us to interact with those angelic presences from whom we receive much guidance and protection. When we are in this state, we invite the angels in, and they in turn answer questions emanating from our depths, questions that we may not have known needed to be asked.

It seems that the human psyche is so constructed that the discovery or creation of unity in the internal world produces a sense of wholeness or unity in the outer world; it's like a mirror reflection. This is what is meant by the New Age saying, "You create your own reality." Outer happenings and inner experience interact with one another. Mind and matter are not only inseparable; they affect one another. Thus, when the inner plane is in harmony with itself, the outer world seems to follow suit, almost magically.

We do not know for certain *how* and *why* this works, but the evidence suggests that communion with the inner self aligns us with the cosmos, with the right and natural order of all things. One might say that we are deliberately getting in tune with the harmonic chords of the universe. And when we are in tune, we produce effects.

Recognizing the Presence of an Angel

Be on the alert. If you feel the presence of an angel, become still and wait for a message. As you become more and more aware of their presence, you will draw them closer and experience them more often. Many of them are coming closer to the human realm in this period of the birth of a new age. They are coming to serve as a bridge between our many individual souls and the ultimate cosmic consciousness that is ready to manifest in all who are ready to receive its energy and message of love and peace to all everywhere. Listen with your ears, eyes, mind, emotions, body, and—above all—your heart.

If you travel without an inner stillness, you are at risk of being cut off from the wisdom of angel guidance. But once you allow yourself to claim your right to be silent, to enjoy solitude, you will be able to sense the presence of the angels and hear them singing.

Working with Breath

Angels, we are told, are pure spirit, and we can enhance our connection to that world simply by using breath techniques (*breath* is synonymous with *spirit*). God "blew upon the waters and the world was created." By becoming aware of our breathing, we become aware of our spiritual nature, for breath is life. Thus, we can use our life breath, as a yogi does, to elevate our consciousness to the realm where the angels dwell.

Breath is the gateway to the sacred angelic dimension. It is something we take for granted, for we could hardly function if we had to consciously remember to breathe. Most of us are unaware of our breathing until it becomes impaired, by a cold or by shortness of breath. When we become aware of our breathing, we connect to the link we have with our spiritual selves. Awareness and control of breath allows us to consciously open ourselves to our innate sacred realm.

Most Eastern philosophies teach that we live in a sea of vital energy and that we absorb and activate this with our breath. The Hindu yogi tradition calls this energy prana. Oriental mind-body balancing techniques such as acupuncture and shiatzu refer to this vital force as Qi (chi). The Hawaiian Huna tradition calls it mana (mana loa in its highest form). In the Hawaiian language, the word *mana-o* means "to think."

Working with breath is a form of spiritual practice. Controlled breathing permits us to extract new energy from the air. Our physical bodies can store this energy in the same way food is stored as fat. When this subtle energy is in short supply, you feel down, listless, and tired, and you can become ill. When it is in abundant supply, you feel "up," energized, optimistic, and full of energy. Though the energy is subtle, it is very real.

You can prove this to yourself by paying attention to the ion content of the air you breathe. Air is charged with positive and negative ions, and a surplus of the former results in an oppressively heavy atmosphere, like that before a thunderstorm. Positive ions sap our energy. Think of how you feel when a storm is brewing and the sky lowers darkly. Negative ions release uplifting energy into the air. When the storm breaks and the rain comes pelting down, the air is clear and refreshed. Your spirits lift, and your mood brightens. You feel energized and ready to go. Proper deep breathing has the effect of saturating your system with negative ions, contributing to the release of tension and to mental calmness, the state in which angels visit upon you.

This energy is subtle, but it is real. Yogis claim that it not only gives vitality to the body but that it also nourishes the spiritual self. A high content of prana in the system causes the unfolding of natural abilities—mental, physical, emotional, and spiritual. Prana is there whether or not we are aware of it. But when we make a deliberate effort to increase it, blocked channels of information open up. The breath is a powerful tool for bringing forth the sacred dimension in ourselves. Conscious breathing develops a communication link between body and mind, between conscious and unconscious, between spirit and angels.

Relaxation

Another important clue to being able to recognize angelic presences is the ability to *relax*. When we are in a state of tension, which is the habitual condition of most of us, we wouldn't be able to recognize an angel if it poked us in the eye with a beam of heavenly light.

Most of us are just too busy to leave uncluttered time and space open for an angel to enter into. We lead lives dominated by such hectic schedules that relaxation seems to evade us most of the time. Why? The answer is not completely clear, but clues can be found in our outlook on life. When we look upon life as an adversary or threat, we are in a perpetual state of "fight-or-flight." Instead of releasing the tension when danger is past, we store it; this retention results in a dangerous buildup that can bring on stress-related disease such as high blood pressure, ulcers, and the like. It seems almost superfluous to add that in such a state, the gentle presence of an angel will go unnoticed.

In the late 1960s, Harvard cardiologist Herbert Benson was involved in some physiologic tests on meditators. He discovered that relaxation methods, of which there are many, caused both psychological and *physiological* changes that served to counterbalance the body's response to "fight-or-flight." He called this the "relaxation response." Not a technique but a coordinated series of internal changes occurring when the mind and body become calm and tranquil, the relaxation response can be achieved by numerous means, including deep breathing, muscle relaxation, meditation, visualization, and prayer. The simplest of these is called "focused meditation." Benson's tests showed that persons who simply sat quietly with their minds focused on a single word, idea, or thought could markedly change their physiology, decreasing metabolism, slowing heart and respiratory rates, and exhibiting brain waves comparable to the dream state. We already have shown that the dream state is a prime source of angelic communications, as are the altered states of consciousness we tend to call a "brown study," or reverie.

Physical relaxation can be an important adjunct to a spiritual practice. Using a relaxation technique regularly will make you more aware of the soft tread of an angel's feet or the beat of angelic wings.

Breathing Relaxation

This is a simple technique that takes only a little time. Sit or lie down in a safe and comfortable spot where there are no distractions. Loosen any tight clothing; unbutton or untie anything that is restrictive on your body. Begin to breathe *consciously*, following your breath in and out of your lungs. Breathe in through the nostrils and out through the mouth. Pay full attention to your breath, in and out, in and out. Listen to the sound and feel the rhythmic pulsing of it. Continue this until you begin to feel calm and relaxed, a state usually signaled by the breath becoming slow and even.

You can deepen your relaxation using breath by imagining that you are breathing in prana, or the vital force of life, and exhaling all tension and negative feeling or experience. One way to do this is to choose one color for the prana and another color for the negative energy and then to see a stream of the positive color coming into your body as you inhale and a stream of the negative color flowing out of you as you exhale. White and black are easy; white is the pure energy of light; and black represents any dark thoughts. But feel free to use the colors that represent to you the positive and the negative energy. Don't worry if distracting thoughts arise. Let them float away (you can tell them you will attend to their needs later) like soap bubbles in the air and return your attention to your breathing.

"The man who has seen the rising moon break out of the clouds at midnight, has been present like an archangel at the creation of light and of the world.

—Ralph Waldo Emerson

To My Friend on the Death of His Sister

With silence only as
their benediction
God's angels come
Where, in the shadow
of a great affliction,
The soul sits dumb.

—John Greenleaf Whittier

CHAPTER 5

Communicating with Angels

The more alert and open you are to receiving communications from angelic energies, the more likely you are to invite in these extraordinary experiences. And the more receptive you become—maintaining a state of constant alertness for their presences—the more likely it is you will find them in your life at some time or other. By expecting a miracle, and by being prepared to recognize one when it occurs, you won't be likely to miss that angelic communication. If you are alert and you feel the presence of an angel, become still and wait for a message. As you become more and more aware of their presence when they visit, you will draw them closer and experience them more often.

Many of them are coming closer to the human realm in this birth of a new age. They are coming to serve as a bridge between ourselves and the ultimate cosmic consciousness that is ready to manifest in all who are ready to receive its energy and message of love and peace to all everywhere. Listen with your ears, eyes, mind, emotions, body, and—above all—heart.

Angels are everywhere. You might not see them, but you can always sense them. And when you begin to have contact with them, such experiences are likely to occur frequently. There are many ways to contact angels.

Invoking the Angels

To call forth an angel or a spirit, practice this invocation. First, enter your sacred space and sit in silence and stillness. Center yourself. Then ask the spirits to come forth. As you say the words, imagine that you see a beautiful white angel with its wings spread protectively.

Angels have long been associated with the four corners, or the four directions, or the four elements. As you speak the invocations, stand facing the direction indicated.

Angels of Fire (West)

I call upon the Angels of Fire to bring love, protection, and safety. May the warmth of the lifegiving fire come into my being and guide me. May the strength of the sun come to me and illuminate me on my way.

Angels of Earth (North)

I call upon the Angels of Earth to bring love, protection, and safety. May the regenerative and restorative power of the earth ground me and guide my way. May the renewing power of the moon come to me and light my path.

Angels of Air (East)

I call upon the Angels of Air to bring love, protection, and safety. May the gentle winds of heaven blow always and imbue me with their airborne energies. May the communication power of Mercury come to me and guide my way.

Angels of Water (South)

I call upon the Angels of Water to bring love, protection, and safety. May the waters of heaven cleanse and purify me. May the flowing and regenerative powers of water come to me and guide my way.

Angels for Specific Needs

To invoke an angel for a specific purpose, concentrate your thoughts on that purpose and perform appropriate rituals. For example, if you want to call forth an angel for your home, especially if you have just moved into a new place, first do a thorough cleaning of the premises. Always get rid of what you don't need, don't use, or don't like. Angels are repelled by unnecessary clutter; it inhibits their freedom of movement and entry. And, quite naturally, they appreciate being invited into a clean environment, just as any guest would.

Before your perform any invocation, decide just what spot or area is the center, or heart, of the situation or matter. If the home is the center, choose the area of the home that seems appropriate. For some, the family room is the heart-center of the house, for others, the kitchen, and so on. Once you have located the center—even if it is not a material space but an inner condition, such as your desire for a happy marriage, or a child, or a new job, sit in perfect silence and stillness for a few minutes, visualizing an angel coming forth at your request. Imagine this angel beaming a beautiful bright white light at you from its head. Ask for the blessing or help you desire. Afterwards, thank the angel for coming.

Writing to Angels

Another way to contact angels is through letter writing. Writing to the angels is a wonderful way to align with their energies and connect with them, and writing them will allow you to gain clarity on your personal issues. When you write to the angels, you establish a mind-heart link between them and you.

Angels of Fire would bring more active love energy, protect outdoor adventures, and make safe courses of action. Angels of Earth would bring more stable love energy, protect the home and family, and make safe the hearth, childbirth, or feminine concerns. Angels of Air would bring more variable love energy, protect intellectual pursuits, and make safe enterprises having to do with air, such as flying. Angels of Water would bring more spiritual love, protect creative pursuits, and make safe anything having to do with water, such as boating or taking a cruise.

You can write to your personal angel, or you can write to all the different kinds of angels. Also, you can write to angels on behalf of other people or about other people. For example, if you are uncertain about how someone feels about you, you can write and ask that person's angel for clarification. Or if a person is ill, you can write and ask his or her angel for healing.

Angel letters are no different that letters you write to friends: Just begin with the salutation "Dear Angel of . . . ." It's always a good idea to do a breathing relaxation exercise to center yourself before writing to an angel. It's best to write in silence and solitude—though I've written letters to angels on airplanes and in hospital waiting rooms filled with people. Angels aren't bothered by exterior noise so much, but they don't like mind-noise interfering with the communication. Try to keep your celestial hot line free of static.

When writing, don't be intimidated by the blank sheet of paper. Just let the words flow from your heart. Don't worry about grammar, spelling, punctuation, or writing style, your angel is your spiritual guide, not your English teacher. Date your letter, give thanks in advance for the answer, and sign it. You won't need a stamp!

Then make your own angel postbox. It can be any kind of a receptacle, even a shoe box covered in pretty paper. Or, you can put the letter under your pillow or in a place where you keep special mementos. Once you have "mailed" your angel letter, put it out of your mind. Don't hang about worrying when you'll get an answer. It will come at the appropriate time and in the appropriate manner.

Special Angelic Colors

Angels have special colors. You can either wear the appropriate color when writing or use paper in the color of the angel to whom you are writing.

Rose, soft green—Guardian angels of the home
Deep sapphire blue—Healing angels
Sky blue—Angels of maternity and birth
White—Ceremonial angels; music angels
Apple Green—Nature angels
Yellow—Angels of art and beauty

Journal Writing

Angel journals provide another way to contact angels. In fact, keeping a journal about your angels is a spiritual practice. Such a journal can tell you where you have been, and show you where you are going. It can serve as a channel into your higher self.

At times when life seems like a lonely trek through an unknown and unpopulated wilderness, an angel journal can offer wonderful companionship. It is truly a friend. Often people say to me, when they learn that I write books, "You should write about me. My life would make a great book." And it is true. Everyone's life would make a great book, and everyone should write the book of his or her life to honor our uniqueness.

Such writing puts you in touch with your celestial helpers because it clears out the "fore-brain chatter"—that never-ending inner dialogue we have with ourselves, mostly criticizing our faults—that interferes with clear reception from your angels. Talk to your angels as you would talk to a trusted confidante whose advice you trust.

Think of your angel journal as "The Book of My Life" and consider it a friend who will always be there to heal, uplift, and celebrate with you. Going back to pages you have written in the past can be an illuminating experience. You may wonder if the person who wrote those lines a few weeks ago was really you.

An angel journal is a marvelous tool for just about any purpose you want it to serve, be it companionship, a place to spill your thoughts and feelings, a friend who will keep your secrets, a factual record, or the telling of your inner life.

Remember that angels are beings of communication; when you write with them in mind, they come closer and align and connect with you. Keeping an angel journal will strengthen your relationship with your guardian angel and celestial best friend. It's a way of keeping in touch, just as you'd telephone your mother or write to a distant friend.

Your angel journal will allow you to communicate with the many layers of yourself, to experiment with forms of expression, and to mirror your many facets. A superb exploratory vehicle, writing about your life's experiences, both inward and outward, can bring fascinating insights and be full of delightful surprises, as well as connect you with your celestial partner, who is interested in all the facets of your life, both light and dark.

To begin an angel journal, you don't need much, just a pen and some paper, a private space if it is available, perhaps a lighted candle or some incense. But these enhancements aren't necessary. I know people who can write in the middle of a traffic jam. One man carries his notebook in his glove compartment just for that purpose. He says writing about angels while those about him are "losing it" keeps him calm and collected. Others comfortably write while commuting on a train or bus.

The charm of angel writing is that it is entirely private. You can think of this activity as a way of manifesting into concrete reality all the thought forms and feelings that float around inside you. No matter where you are in your life—at the beginning, in the middle, or near the end—I would encourage you to begin an angel journal, lest you miss them unawares!

Whatever you are doing now, wherever you are in your life, you are on a spiritual quest. You may call it something else–a search for meaning, finding yourself, or getting in touch with what you really want to do in life. Labels are unimportant. The spiritual quest is life, and life is a spiritual quest. It is the center, the still point at the hub of the turning wheel of fortune, out of which all else comes, and the angels are our companions and helpers on this quest.

Remember that there is a special angel for every day of the week. You can address your letters or communications to these angels on their own days. There is also a special angel for every hour of each day of the week! That's too many angels to list here, but you don't have to address them by name; they'll know. You can send a celestial e-mail to the angel of 2:00 P.M. on Friday if, say, you have a presentation to make at that time, or a medical procedure scheduled.

The real core of our spirit is tucked away in the corners of everyday life. We can sense an angel presence when we are diapering the baby, washing the car, taking a shower, vacuuming the rug, building a shelf, raking the lawn, or shopping for groceries. Angels accompany us when we stand in line at the bank, make a travel reservation, eat at a restaurant, or spend the day lounging around at home. Although angels do appear in extraordinary circumstances (the ones we most often hear about), the co-mingling of the inner, private self with the details of life's commonplace activities is the means by which we most often meet angels. It is in this living of our everyday lives that we find the spirit—the real soul food that nourishes us.

Our angel journal, and the keeping of it as a record, is a transformational process not unlike what artists undergo as they work on the material that forms their artwork while simultaneously working on the needs of their souls. By following our soul-directedness–what I call the "internal imperative"–we keep on the course that will fulfill who we truly are, without the societal and personal-traumatic overlays that have obscured the gold of our authentic selves.

Many of today's angel books are now filled with the recollections of those who have had angel encounters, but have heretofore kept quiet about them. Ordinary people living ordinary lives are "coming out of the closet" about angels and how they interact with our lives. Moreover, they are writing about these experiences.

Writing is a sorting process. It is also a great teacher. A dialogue with an angel is never dull or uninteresting. Once you get to know your angel, your deeper levels will become activated. And you will have the ultimate reward of actually experiencing your own life firsthand, not just living vicariously through TV and newspaper accounts of others people's stories about meeting and conversing with angels!

Please lay aside your fears that somehow you won't get it right. There's no right or wrong. You can have terrible handwriting or be a master at calligraphy. You can be a high school dropout or possess a doctorate in literature. And if you lack writing skills, what better way to improve them? Write. That's all. And don't worry about the details. Just put them down as you see fit. You can also draw angels as you picture them, or as you have seen them, and paste in cutouts of angel pictures if that pleases you. If you like structure, be neat and orderly. If you don't, scribble any old way, so long as you can read it.

The Monitoring Technique

As we go about our daily lives, we usually are in a blur of automatic, preprogrammed thoughts and activities. Our mental processes most of the time are like a slightly out of focus photograph. We ordinarily only go into sharp focus in times of crisis. As a result, we are often bored and "not there." So much of our everyday life is such a blur of routine that we miss what our angels are trying to tell us. To combat this tendency, I have developed and teach a technique I call monitoring, which is a way of consciously focusing on the day's input, either as it is happening or during brief periods of reflection.

If the idea of learning to monitor your thoughts and feelings at first seems daunting, do not let that prevent you from attempting it. Like learning to ride a bicycle, it at first will seem clumsy and impossible and then, suddenly—bingo!—you will be off and away with ease.

Begin by consciously storing in memory your thoughts, feelings, and reactions with regard to the events of the day. If you have trouble remembering them, train yourself to take brief notes during the day, either during or after their occurrence. Note the particulars of the situation, along with your reactions. A few words will do; you will develop a kind of shorthand in time. The purpose is to jog your memory later and enable you to recall the entire event, complete with "feeling tone."

When thoughts and feelings arise from the inner self, do not ignore them or push them away; record them either mentally or physically so that they do not vanish in the well of forgetfulness. During the day, whenever you have a spot of unoccupied time–waiting for a bus, sitting on a train, standing in line–review what you have noted to fix it firmly for later evaluation.

At the end of the day, set aside a few minutes of time to examine the entire day's input for clues to messages from angels. Record your thoughts and feelings along with any physical or environmental circumstances.

In time, you will perceive patterns of meaning. Your life is not an accidental or random event; it has meaning and purpose. Keeping an angel journal will help you to discover this.

If you are new to journal keeping, you may need some time to acclimate yourself to writing about your angelic experiences on a regular basis. One friend makes it a habit to write down a self-created angel prayer every day. Here is a sample prayer:

"Dear Angel–Be with me today and keep me safe. Let me be aware of your presence around me."

Use any form of journal you please. I find a bound notebook is best, as I tend to lose separate pieces of paper. A simple spiral notebook is inexpensive, or you may prefer a cloth-bound book.

Rereading what you have written either the next day or even a year later can be an illuminating experience. For one thing, you won't forget any of your angel messages and experiences! Enjoy your angel journal; think of it as a dear friend with whom you spend intimate time.

Write when and for as long and as much as it suits you each time. If you are a person who responds well to a scheduled activity, by all means put it in your schedule. If not—and I think this preferable—let your writing be spontaneous. Whatever works for you at the time is best.

In addition to keeping your journal on a regular basis, you can benefit by writing out your feelings about any particularly experience, angelic or otherwise. James W. Pennebaker, Ph.D., a professor in the Department of Psychology at Southern Methodist University, developed an effective technique in which you spend 20 minutes writing nonstop and without concern about spelling or grammar. If you do this, emotions will likely pour forth, even tears—but these are tears of release. This is an excellent method to gain insight into the meaning of your life.

Your angel journal can also be a way to help lessen stress and handle anxiety or depression. Making a commitment to writing on a regular basis is the key to success.

Here are some helpful angel writing tips:

- Decide whether to write by hand or keyboard.
- If by hand, select loose-leaf paper or a bound book.
- Choose a book that opens flat.
- Decide whether to use lined or unlined paper.

- The writing implement you use should be one that is permanent and does not smear. You may want to keep a special pen or pencil just for this purpose.
- If using a keyboard, you can use paper that is three-hole punched and keep your pages in a ring binder. Or, you can create a file folder or a computer file.
- Browse in a stationery store for an assortment of pens, markers, and colored pencils, and use them for a variety of moods and experiences. One client writes all her dreams in purple.

Make a Covenant with Your Angel Journal

Think for a few minutes about your purpose in keeping a journal and whether you are willing to make a commitment to writing regularly. Then put your thoughts onto paper. Study what you have written and see whether you are satisfied with your purpose; if you are not, make changes. Your statement of purpose might go something like this:

> *I'm keeping my angel journal for the purpose of getting in touch with my Angels who guard and guide me, with the aim of generating more consciousness.*
>
> *My goal is to become more aware of messages from my angels and to act on this information for my spiritual growth and development.*
>
> *I believe that keeping a journal will aid this process by providing me*

with a framework in which I can record and reflect upon my experiences and wherein I can chart my progress.

Consciousness

"We learn to live consciously through becoming aware of inner and outer events as they are happening. Building a conscious self means becoming increasingly aware of inner events, bodily events, and interpersonal events. A conscious self is able to experience in full awareness all the distinctly different components of the self, including feelings, needs, drives, and values. A conscious self lives consciously."

—Gershen Kaufman and Lev Raphael,
The Dynamics of Power

Consciousness is our most precious possession. Without it, we are mere robots, only going through the motions of life, not really living. In the ability to think, reflect, and wonder, we possess treasures greater than those found in all the tombs of Egypt, or the immense riches of the Orient, or the vast diamond mines of South Africa. Without consciousness, we do not know who we are and cannot find out. This greatest of gifts should be guarded carefully and used wisely. The human mind can observe itself thinking–subject and object simultaneously. We can "see" ourselves doing what we do. Consciousness is the inner companion who never goes away. It is even attested that some surgical patients emerge from under anesthesia with memories of what happened in the operating room. The reason for this is simple: Consciousness is *always there*, at some level.

The purpose of angelic communications to the pilgrim on a spiritual journey is a consciousness-raising mission. As we progress along the Way, consciousness emerges into the light of spirituality, and we become aware not only of our true selves but also that others possess true selves, and we want to know those selves, not the false ones we are most often presented with. The emerging of consciousness is like the peeling away of the layers of an onion.

It takes consciousness of "all the distinctly different components of the self" to make us aware of the whisperings of angel guidance. So often our angel guidance is drowned out by the noise—both external and internal—with which we surround ourselves. Consciousness thrives in the silence of reflection.

The angel message may reach us merely as a vague sensation, either mental or emotional.

It can be a tension or a sense that something is about to happen. Consciousness may register as no more than an ephemeral state of being, like the feeling that one has forgotten something important but cannot for the life of one remember what it is. Ideas communicated to us by our angels may come to us as feelings, or we may find ourselves undergoing a change in values as the result of a crisis.

When we listen and pay attention to "the still small voice," we find angel guidance is available. The directions we need most often come from within, yet they can be mirrored by what is happening without. The question is, How can we sort through our multiplicity of feelings, sensations, intuitions, thoughts, and reactions to get to the spiritual core of the matter?

Angels Who Visit in Dreams

The great Swiss psychologist Carl Jung called dreams "the royal road to the unconscious." They are also the gateway to the subtle realms where spirits abide. Sometimes they are like long letters we write to ourselves. A friend of mine says an unremembered dream is "an unopened letter from God."

Dreams speak their own language, and angels who visit in dreams come through that portal to bring their messages, which we often need to interpret. The reason the dream state is so propitious for contacting angels is that it is approximates the way angels function—fluidly, openly, timelessly. When we go to sleep, we let go of the tightly organized, highly regimented linear left-brain thinking that usually dominates our waking hours. While asleep, we have no schedule; we float freely in a magical substance in which swim creatures of the deep and that creates visions of incredible creativity. Dreams are angels' territory.

Dreams of Angels as Guides

During my life, I have encountered many angels who came as guides. You too will have more than one angel during your lifetime, but you can call upon these cosmic tour guides at any time you feel you need guidance.

An angel may appear as an archetype—an old man or a wise woman, a human figure you may or may not recognize, an animal that talks or communicates telepathically, a spiritual entity such as an "intelligence" from another dimension, or even a rock or body of water. These symbols are likely to shift and change over time and with the subject for which you are asking guidance.

For example, asking for guidance with healing may produce a figure consonant with your idea of a healer. Accept what comes, for it arises from your deepest core where your sacred self dwells.

By making the effort to meet and talk with your angel, you will be setting a precedent for getting help on a regular, sometimes unasked-for basis. Your angel can warn you of problems in advance, it can provide you with penetrating insight, and it can reveal subtle nuances of meaning that are imbedded in your everyday experience.

For example, about 15 years ago, I encountered a group of nine men in an exceptionally vivid dream.

The Dream of Green Fire

In this dream, I am in a large house in a wooded area with a young woman friend. Outside, there is a blizzard. I hear my name called. I cannot imagine who would be calling my name late at night with a storm raging, but I know I must go and find out whether someone in trouble needs my help.

Bundling up, I forge out into the snow, in the direction of the voice calling my name. Going through dense woods, I come upon a clearing, surrounded by a ring of green fire. Inside the ring of green fire there is no storm; all is quiet, placid, peaceful, and warm. Nine men robed and hooded like monks, in long woolen olive-brown gowns, tied at the waist with knotted golden ropes, sit in a circle inside the ring of green fire. In the center of the circle there is a small bonfire that glows with the same emerald green light as the fire ring.

By gesture, they invite me to enter the circle. From the maelstrom of the raging storm, I step into this center of absolute calm, safety, and warmth. A great sense of peace descends over me, as if I have at long last come home. Beneath their hoods I can see their faces; all are very old, wrinkled, and wizened, and have deep, dark eyes like pools of unfathomable wisdom. I feel a sense of protection coming from them.

One rises and steps toward me, and I see that he has my cat, Fuzz, cradled in his arms. I realize that the voice I heard calling my name was that of my precious Fuzz, who was lost in the terrible storm and needed rescuing. He is handed to me ceremoniously, like a gift on an important occasion. I can tell he is perfectly all right and has suffered no injuries from the traumatic experience of being lost in the cold and snow. Taking him from the monk's wrinkled old hands, I feel a sense of complete and utter peace and safety.

When I awoke from the dream, I pondered the symbolism, and the answer came immediately: Fuzz was my heart. They had told me that my heart—most fearfully broken more than once, in essence lost in the dark cold—had been rescued and kept safe. In the dream it was returned to me intact and healed.

The nine men appeared to me several different times over the next several years, always accompanied by ice and snow, to which they

were immune and within which they created a warm center. Though they appeared to be human, I knew they were from the angel world.

In another dream, they gave me a large book made of parchment sheaves, ancient and yellowed but not fragile, the pages covered with a mysterious writing that I could not decipher but that I understood to be important esoteric knowledge. I realized that the nine men were celestial sages from the world of no time. I came to call them The Council of Nine. Later, I was inspired to write a poem, "The Return," about the experience of this wondrous group.

When I read Betty Eadie's *Embraced by the Light,* I was astonished to find that one chapter was entitled "The Council of Men." In her vision, she met 12 men, seated around a kidney-shaped table, who radiated "absolute love" to her. She also learned from this council of men many fascinating things about herself and her life. In addition, she describes three men who meet her at the beginning of her near-death experience. The numbers 12, 9, and 3 are all related, each being divisible by the core number 3. The number 3 represents the trinity, or the triangle, of mind-body-spirit and the threefold nature of divinity, of great symbolic importance and spiritual significance. The number 9 represents completion, humanitarianism, and universal compassion. The number 12, which is the number of the signs of the zodiac, reduces back to 3 using the numerological formula 12 = 1 + 2 = 3.

We are all capable of experiencing contact with our own deeper dimensions symbolically. It is through the use of symbols that we can connect with what cannot be seen, heard, touched, tasted, or smelled. Whatever symbolic form your angelic guides take will depend on which forms you are most open to and able to respond to. In my case, these symbolic forms often have to do with art and books.

Other Altered State Experiences

It's even possible for one person to receive guidance from another person's angel. I had such an experience when I first began to practice astrology professionally. My friend, Josephine Corado, a blind psychic, had invited me to spend the weekend at her home on Long Island and had arranged for me to read the charts of several of her clients. I arrived on a Friday afternoon carrying some astrology books. At that time, I was accustomed to spending three or four hours of preparation time on each chart, and although I had prepared most of the charts I was to read over the weekend, one remained undone.

That evening as we sat chatting in Jo's living room–she in the recliner and me on the couch–she suddenly burst out laughing.

"What's so funny?" I asked in puzzlement.

"Akenaton," she replied. "He's standing right in front of you."

I knew Akenaton was what she called her angel, but there was nothing in front of me but the coffee table.

"Where?" I asked, looking around.

"Right *there*," she pointed a finger to the spot where my tummy was.

"What does he want with me?" I asked perplexedly.

"I haven't the faintest idea," was her unhelpful reply.

Shortly after this conversation, she announced that she was going to bed early because she didn't feel well. I reminded her that I had a chart to prepare the next morning before my first reading at noon, and she promised to get me up by 9:00 A.M. It was about 10:00 P.M when she retired, and as I'm a late-night person, I was at loose ends to occupy myself. Since Jo was blind, there were no books and no TV. I wasn't in the mood to study astrology, the only books I had. I lay on the couch to meditate.

As I lay there, wide awake but very relaxed, a curious thing happened. My entire body began to vibrate as if someone had plugged me into an electric socket. It was very intense, though not actually uncomfortable. The source of the sensation seemed to be the center of my forehead (where the "third eye" is located). I didn't understand at all what was happening to me, but as I was in what I knew to be a spiritually saturated atmosphere, I made no effort to

get up. The room was not dark; there was a streetlight just outside the uncurtained window. I looked about myself, but I saw nothing out of the ordinary.

The sensation finally stopped—*three hours later*. As unexpectedly and inexplicably as it had started, it stopped, like the switching off of a light. Whatever circuit I had been connected to went dead. I felt none the worse for the experience, and I got up and went to bed. In the morning as promised, Jo woke me and I sat at her dining-room table to prepare the chart. I worked away, consulting my books only occasionally, and when I had finished, I asked Jo, who had a talking watch, for the time. "It's 9:45," she told me.

I knew this could not be right, for I had finished three hours' worth of work, and I had not started until a bit after 9:00 A.M. "That's

impossible," I said. "Could you check your watch again?" She came over to me and held out her wrist and I heard a little mechanical voice say, "Nine forty-six." How could that be? I wondered. I had not felt any sense of time speeded up, had worked at my usual slow and thorough pace, or so I thought, and yet I was done. To make sure, I called the time service. Then I remembered the previous evening's strange experience and Jo's having told me her angel was standing in front of me. Could there be a connection?

In the weeks that followed, it became evident to me that I had a far greater understanding and knowledge of astrology than I had before I went to Long Island that weekend. At a conference at which I was a lecturer, a thoroughly seasoned astrologer who had been practicing for 20 years came up to me and said that

I was the "best technical astrologer" she knew. Amazed, I understood that I had received a powerful teaching that night, like an intravenous injection straight into the brain. Since then, my readings have risen to a level of comprehension that still amazes me, for I know that I didn't earn the knowledge I have, that it was a gift from an angel. Is there an Angel of Astrology?

Qualities of Angels

Angels of different qualities have revealed themselves to me. For example, during one period, when I was studying the Tarot, I received information and guidance through specific sounds. I identified three different energies, one of which was a thin, high-pitched tone, barely audible but piercing nonetheless. The second was lower, but still in the high range, and seemed to cover a slightly wider band of the sound spectrum.

The third sound was much lower, almost a bass, and broader. Each of these sounds conveyed a different type of information.

For example, when I heard the highest note, I knew it was time to sit quietly and meditate, that a "message" was coming in through this vibration. These sounds occurred at all times of the day and night, in my home as well as other places. They seemed to follow me around. So be aware that you can receive guidance from angels in many guises.

Here is a method for making contact with an angel guide. You can do this anytime you feel the need. One angel guide may stay with you for a long or a short time. You may meet different angels at different periods of your life. There is no right or wrong way to contact a angel, although some do appear spontaneously without your asking.

In the following meditation, you are going to meet someone whom you can trust and rely on. To prepare yourself, do the following:

1. Articulate a question you wish to ask your angel. Formulate the question clearly and succinctly. Vague questions beget vague answers. Be specific.
2. Do not ask a question requiring a yes or no answer. The purpose is to make contact with your angel.
3. Stick to your present situation; avoid generalities.
4. Do not ask a question requiring a prediction. This is usually interpreted as lack of faith. Asking for guidance is always good. State the subject about which you wish to receive angelic guidance.
5. Be willing to trust your angel and to take whatever form appears to you. If you

draw a blank, try again later when you are more relaxed.

6. When your angel appears, pay attention to how he or she looks. Ask your angel for a name or a symbol by which you can recognize him or her in the future.

After you have prepared yourself for your encounter with your guide, find the time to be alone and undisturbed for half an hour. Using any of the breathing and/or relaxation methods already given, relax completely and let go of the day's tensions and cares.

Mentally take yourself to a place somewhere in nature—a forest, the seaside, a flower-filled meadow, a lakeshore, a cove, a wood—whatever appeals to you. See in front of you, in this pleasant place, a veiled object, full of mystery. A puff of wind may come along and blow away the covering, and your angel will be revealed to you. Take whatever image comes and begin to engage in a dialogue with it. Ask your question and wait for an answer. If one doesn't come at once, be patient. The answer may come in words, through intuition, or telepathically, as an image, even as a snatch of song or an instruction to read a book or magazine article.

The specifics are not as important as making the contact. Whatever springs into your mind is the right answer. Your angels are in touch with the deepest part of your being, which is connected to all reality everywhere at all times and places.

When you have met your angel, introduce yourself, and ask your question. Notice the details of the place so that you can return here whenever you like. Fix it in your memory. When you get the answer to your question, thank your angel and say you will look forward to future meetings.

If you do not get an answer, or if the answer doesn't seem to make sense, accept that also and try again later. Remember, you are learning a new skill.

"Angels cannot directly determine acts of the human will. The inviolability of its freedom exempts it from such determination either by angels or by men. But just as one human being can influence the will of another by efforts at persuasion, or by motivating it in one way or another through arousing emotions, so angels have even greater power to influence the will of individuals in these indirect ways."

—Mortimer J. Adler, *The Angels and Us*

The Other World

Sweet souls around us
watch us still,
Press nearer to our side;
Into our thought, into our
prayers,
With gentle helpings glide.

—Harriet Beecher Stowe

CHAPTER 6

Angels in Art and Literature

Softly and gently, dearly ransomed soul
In my most loving arms I now enfold thee,
And, o'er the penal waters, as they roll,
I poise thee, and I lower thee, and
hold thee.
And carefully I dip thee in the lake,
And then, without a sob or a resistance,
Dost through the flood thy rapid
passage take,
Sinking deep, deeper, into the dim distance.
Angels, to whom the willing task is given
Shall tend, and nurse, and lull thee, as
thou liest;
And Masses on the earth, and prayers
in heaven,
Shall aid thee at the throne of the
Most Highest.
Farewell, but not for ever! brother dear,
Be brave and patient on thy bed of sorrow,

Swiftly shall pass thy night of trial here,
And I will come and wake thee on the
morrow.

—Dom Wilmart, *Auteurs spirituels et textes dévots*

Angels have a long tradition in art and literature. However, depictions of them in stone are the first forms of angel art we know. As history begins to be recorded we find images of them in many cultures around the world. These suggest that the notion of angels is embedded in our psyches.

The Art of Michael

Michael, the Prince of the Heavenly Hosts, is always pictured in Renaissance paintings as young, strong, handsome, and wearing armor. He is supposed to be God's champion or chief warrior as well as the protector general of the Roman Catholic Church. Michael is also known as the patron saint of the Hebrew nation, but the Jewish tradition forbids images or icons, so there's no Jewish religious art. The same is true of Islam, which forbids idolatry of images and which, therefore, has developed astonishingly beautiful geometric art forms to be viewed symbolically rather than literally.

Raphael, The Sociable Archangel

In the canvases of such masters as Botticelli, Lorrain, Pollajuolo, Ghirlandaio, Titan, and Rembrandt, Raphael is variously pictured holding a pilgrim's staff and a fish, or as a winged saint dining with Adam and Eve. Milton calls him the "sociable archangel" in *Paradise Lost,* which may be a reference to his journey as a companion to Tobias.

Halos and Wings

In Christian art from the 12th century onward (that with which we are most familiar), angels almost always wear halos, though halos are not mentioned in Scripture as being part of standard angel gear. The halo is found in ancient Buddhist art and was also used in Greco-Roman art to indicate gods and heroes. In the fourth century, Christian artists adopted the use of a halo to float over the heads of Jesus, angels, and saints, presumably to indicate that these were supernatural beings, different from humans.

Much sculpture and stained glass windows were part of Christian art, and these magnificent cathedrals that seem to rise up into the very heavens were graced with beautiful depictions of the entire Christian story and included a plentitude of angels and angelic hosts. (It is important to remember that in this era, before Gutenberg's invention of the printing press, the populace was largely illiterate, and the stained glass windows were there not only for aesthetic reasons, but also to educate believers in the story of their faith.) For example, the angels surrounding the main portal of the cathedral at Chartres, France, are there to express the sense of perfection of God's creation as well as the sense humans had developed of angels being their protectors and guides or guardians.

The question of wings is still a matter of debate. Few of us today would imagine a wingless angel—unless, of course, it appeared in human or animal form—because the image of the winged angel has been burned into our consciousness by centuries of beautiful and compelling art, much of it painted or sculpted by great masters, who represented angels with wings most magnificent. Curiously, however, even though Scripture speaks of angels flying—in Daniel 9:21, Gabriel is said to come to Daniel "in swift flight," and in Revelation 14:6–7, Gabriel flies again—there is no specific mention of wings per se.

Dante Alighieri's classic epic, *The Divine Comedy (Purgatory)*, gives a vivid description of an angel at the helm of a boat, his wings flared upward, acting as sails, ferrying souls to their destination. Dante calls the angel "the Bird of God." By now, angels and wings go together like coffee and cream, or Christmas and decorations. For this, we have primarily the great artist of the

Renaissance, Raphael (no doubt named for the great archangel), to thank. He painted countless canvasses (a great many of them in the Vatican) of ethereal looking angels with fluffy, feathery wings. These rather blurry representations are quite dreamlike, as befits the angelic realm.

The Great Artists and Angels

Rubens's Procession of Cherubs

Peter Paul Rubens, the great and extremely prolific Flemish painter (1577–1640) was especially fond of sacred subjects. One of his masterworks, *Apotheosis of James I,* which hangs in the banquet hall of Whitehall in London, filling the long side panels, shows a procession of cherubs.

Rembrandt

In *Paradise Lost*, John Milton equates the archangel Gabriel with the chief of the angelic guards placed over Paradise. Gabriel is credited as the angel in the famous wrestling encounter with Jacob (though different sources credit Michael, Uriel, Metatron, Samael, and Chamuel with the role of the "dark antagonist"). No matter which angel was responsible for the fight, the famous scene was immortalized in a canvas by Rembrandt.

Rembrandt was continually inspired to paint angels, many of which appear in his larger canvases; there are also glimpses of angels in his multitude of sketches (most of which repose in the Dutch national museum in Amsterdam). In these, the angels are more informal, charming, and approachable, especially the rendering of the archangel Raphael with Tobit, as companion on the journey.

The Pre-Raphaelites

William Blake was followed by a group of artists and writers who named themselves the Pre-Raphaelites. They formed a brotherhood of painters and poets in 1848 in protest against both the prevailing standards of British art and the oncoming rush of the Industrial Revolution, which threatened all handicrafts. They chose the name because their inspiration came from the work of Italian painters that predated Raphael. In etheral tones, the Pre-Raphaelites depicted angels and angelic-like portraits of humans. But they were fated to fade away before the end of the 19th century, and with their passing, angels were eclipsed by the onset of technological "progress" and the new scientific materialism, neither of which needed them, pictorially or otherwise.

Yet, angels remained, carved in stone, etched on copper, painted on canvas; their images can be seen in nearly every city and town of the Western Hemisphere. They grace railway stations and libraries. They are seen on murals and friezes. They decorate war memorials and museum façades and are cast in bronze atop skyscrapers. They float gracefully on the domes of town halls. They are even seen on the walls of department stores, hospitals, and movie theatres. They stand in marble in the middle of park fountains or set upon pedestals in public squares. Wherever you look, you'll see an angel.

Angels in Literature

Dante's *Divine Comedy*

Dante constructed such a towering spire in mere words that it would take an entire volume just to examine and discuss it. One part of the great cathedral in words that Dante created is his "Angelic Orders," derived from the work of Dionysius (or pseudo-Dionysius) the Areopagite.

Dante's *Celestial Hierarchies* compares God to a ray of cosmic light that, although it will always remain the "One," "becomes a manyness," dispersing itself and proceeding into the manifestation of the myriad universe and all in it from largest to tiniest.

This primal ray of light, according to Dante's interpretation of the angelic hierarchies, must be so arranged "that we might be led, each according to his capacity, from the most holy imagery to formless, unific, elevative principles and assimilations." Thus, everything is "delivered in a supermundane manner to Celestial Natures [Angels] . . . given to us in symbols," so that we may attain "our due measure of deification."

In Dante's concept, theophany, which is "a beholding of God which shows the divine likeness, figured in itself as a likeness in form of that which is formless [through which] a divine light is shed upon the seers . . . and they are initiated into some participation of divine things."

In this theological system, the angels are the most potent of theophanies, who, in a top-down manner, pass along God to humanity through all their ranks, from highest to lowest (angels), until it reaches humans via the angels. Thus, one could say that every angelic appearance is in fact an appearance of God in disguise; rather like the Greek god Zeus, who appeared as a swan or a shower of gold because his full glory would incinerate the beholder, the Divine Light must be dimmed for human consumption.

Several centuries later, the French illustrator and painter Paul Gustave Doré (1833–83) would be inspired to create illustrations for Dante's *Divine Comedy*—magnificent, brooding etchings of demons writhing in the pits of hell and gloriously rendered angels—the entire heavenly host spiraling off into the infinite region of the most high.

William Blake

At the time of his death, the English mystic-poet-engraver William Blake (1757–1827) was engaged in designing etchings to illustrate the *Divine Comedy*. Previously, Blake, who etched his own designs on copper plates, using a newly developed technique, had executed and engraved many religious designs for his own lyrical poems. He wrote volumes about his experiences with angels and had great influence upon many of the major thinkers of his time. His munificent legacy bequeathed to the world includes some of the most impassioned drawings of angels to ever come from the hand of an artist. Here is an excerpt from one of his texts:

> *It is not because angels are holier than men or devils that makes them angels, but because they do not expect holiness from one another, but from God alone.*

Richard Crashaw

There exist innumerable paintings, by both masters and lesser artists, of the Annunciation scene, with Gabriel pictured as the angel who brings Mary the "glad tidings." Though pictorial representations of this momentous event abound, verse versions are rare. There is one by the seventh-century English poet Richard Crashaw in his *Steps to the Temple*:

Heavens Golden-winged Herald, late
hee saw
To a poor Galilean virgin sent.
How low the Bright Youth bow'd, and
with what awe
Immortall flowers to her faire hand
present.

John Donne

The English poet John Donne (1573–1631) wrote of angels in his *Sermons on the Psalms and Gospels:* "I throw myself down in my Chamber and I . . . invite God and his angels thither, and when they are there, I neglect and his angels for the noise of a fly, for the rattling of a coash, for the whining of a door."

In his *Devotions*, Donne says, "I consider thy plentiful goodness, O my God, in employing angels more than one, in so many of thy remarkable works." Detailing the many single instances in Scripture in which not a single angel but a whole chorus (or crowd in the case of those ascending and descending Jacob's ladder) are seen, Donne continues, "From the first to their last, are angels, angels in the plural, in every service angels associated with angels."

Longfellow's Angel

In *The Golden Legend,* the American poet Henry Wadsworth Longfellow (1807–82) calls Gabriel "the angel of the moon who brings man the gift of hope."

"And the angel said, 'I have learned that every man lives, not through care for himself, but by love.'"

—Leo Tolstoy